THE BRANNAN PLAN
Farm Politics and Policy

THE BRANNAN PLAN
Farm Politics and Policy

by Reo M. Christenson

GREENWOOD PRESS, PUBLISHERS
WESTPORT, CONNECTICUT

Library of Congress Cataloging in Publication Data

Christenson, Reo Millard, 1918-
   The Brannan plan.

   Reprint of the ed. published by the University of
Michigan Press, Ann Arbor.
   Includes bibliographical references.
   1. Agriculture and state--United States. I. Title.
[HD1761.C5 1974]   338.1'873   74-10728
ISBN 0-8371-7650-6

To my wife, Helen,
whose help and forbearance
made this volume possible

CONTENTS

THE BRANNAN PLAN
Farm Politics and Policy

I

BACKGROUND AND
FORMULATION

On April 7, 1949, the Senate and House committees on agriculture held an extraordinary joint session. Secretary of Agriculture Charles F. Brannan, after months of prodding from the committee chairmen, was finally ready to present the Department's views on national agricultural policy. There was an air of expectancy in the chamber, growing out of the rather singular secrecy which had cloaked departmental planning in recent weeks. Would Brannan endorse Title I of the Agricultural Act of 1948, providing for fixed 90 per cent of parity price supports? Or would he put the weight of his influence behind Title II, establishing a flexible support scale? [1] Or—a few who knew Brannan well wondered—would he come up with something else, something bearing the unmistakable imprint of Charles F. Brannan?

The last group surmised correctly. In the course of his testimony that morning [2] Secretary Brannan proposed an agricultural program which became known as the "Brannan Plan." Employing an "income support" formula largely reflecting the prosperous war and postwar years, Brannan called for the highest level of guaranteed farm price supports in the nation's history. He proposed to extend income protection to farmers producing certain perishable commodities—by means of direct federal cash payments whenever their prices fell below a level dictated by his "income support" formula. He suggested, rather audaciously, that large-scale commercial farmers share the program's benefits only on that part of their production which an efficient "family farm" unit could produce. Finally, he recommended that farmers either abide by approved conservation practices and necessary production or marketing controls or forfeit the program's cash and loan benefits.

The unveiling of the Brannan Plan touched off one of the most vigorous—and vitriolic—political controversies in recent American history. In addition to producing a first-class row in Congress, a bitter feud between the Secretary of Agriculture and the leader of the biggest farm organization, and a major split in the so-called "farm bloc" (which has not yet been repaired), the Brannan Plan provoked a lusty national debate on agricultural policy which brought scores of nonfarm organizations into the fray.

Although the enemies of the Brannan Plan managed to convert the Plan into an epithet, and won a smashing victory over it, many thoughtful students of agriculture have retained a continuing interest in it. They have insisted that one of its central ideas—protecting the farmer from the hazards of the free market by a system of compensatory payments instead of price supports —merits far more serious congressional attention than it has ever received. The bitterness of the battle in 1949–50 has left an emotional residue unfavorable to a calm reconsideration of the Plan, but the persistence with which it has cropped up in discussions of agricultural policy since 1950 suggests that the Plan has potentialities worthy of further study.

For example, the Research and Policy Committee of the Committee for Economic Development, reporting in January, 1956, suggested two general methods of protecting farmers against short-run declines in demand. The second proposal was as follows: "The market price may be allowed to seek its level and supplementary payments made to farmers by the government. The goal would be to stabilize incomes by making a payment to farmers representing some part of the difference between the actual market price and what the normal price would be in a period of high employment and normal yields.

"Depending on the nature of the problem either plan might

work successfully if the level of support is correctly chosen." [3]

Respected agricultural economists John D. Black and James T. Bonnen observed in 1956, "The most constructive program . . . is to let the prices of farm products fall well toward their free market level, and make up the difference between those prices and a level that will insure a near-normal income in the form of direct payments." [4]

Loren Soth, editorial writer of the farm-conscious *Des Moines Register and Tribune,* wrote in 1957: "From a practical economic standpoint, the direct payment method has many advantages, especially and obviously in the case of perishable products. How much more sensible to let the market price sink to whatever level will move all the meat, milk, eggs, potatoes into consumption—and then pay farmers in cash whatever subsidy is deemed necessary! Even in the case of durable products, such as wheat and cotton, once a safe national reserve is in storage, why not let the market price serve its function of adjusting supply and demand—giving producers a direct payment instead of a loan for putting more in storage." [5]

Mr. Soth also observes, "In total cost to the American public such payments to farmers probably would be less than the equivalent subsidy through government buying and storage. Consumers would get their meat and milk at lower prices, which would be an offset against the greater outlay by government." [6]

Summarizing the reports of "sixty specialists from universities, government, national farm organizations and elsewhere," the Subcommittee on Agricultural Policy to the Joint Economic Committee reported in February, 1958, that:

"The principal feasible applications of direct payments appear to be

"(a) Temporary use at modest levels to alleviate short-term, distress situations in markets, especially for perishables. Such use might be helpful in evening out the hog cycle through a forward-pricing system, for example.

"(b) Income support for farmers during depression, when price support and production control might have particularly adverse effects on consumers.

"(c) More or less permanent use, but with restrictions added to avoid stimulation of output." [7]

Economist J. K. Galbraith wrote early in 1957, "A change in farm policy from the system of pegging farm prices to one of allowing them to find their own level, with the farmers' income protected by direct payments, would be immensely useful (in attacking inflation)." [8]

Many other examples might be cited, but these will suffice to demonstrate that although the Brannan Plan was buried alive in 1950, it may yet emerge from the tomb to lead the nation to a sounder farm policy.

The story of how the Brannan Plan was conceived, its elements of strength and weakness, and the circumstances leading to its defeat can illuminate much that needs to be understood about agricultural policy and policy-making in America. If it also suggests the desirability of a dispassionate and judicious re-examination of the Plan in the light of current farm problems, so much the better. Certainly the Brannan Plan embodied several concepts sufficiently bold, imaginative, and appealing to deserve a better fate than it has received to date.

A brief review of the larger outlines of American agricultural policy development since 1932 will help refresh the reader's memory and put the story of the Brannan Plan in sharper focus.

The farmer's position in 1932 was truly a desperate one. As described in the *1940 Yearbook of Agriculture:*

Gross farm income from the production of 1932 was less than half that of 1929, while fixed charges, including taxes and interest, were not proportionately lower. The Department of Agriculture estimated that the average farmer, after paying the expenses of production, rent, interest, and taxes, had only about $230 left out of his year's income . . . All the capital employed in agriculture had a value in January 1933 of only 38 billions of dollars as compared with 58 billions in 1929 and 79 billions in 1919, while farm debt remained virtually unchanged. [9]

In one year sixty thousand farmers were driven from their homes, unable to pay the mortgage installments on their farms.

Those who were once convinced that surpluses would vanish if only the farm marketing co-operatives were given free rein were now disillusioned. Confidence that the foreign market could absorb American surpluses was also dying away. The abrupt curtailment of our extraordinary foreign lending operations in the late 1920's, logically coinciding with the onset of the world depression, gave the *coup de grâce* to the notion that we could export our surpluses (and with them, our economic troubles) to foreign lands. Finally, the costly failure of the Federal Farm Board's Surplus Purchase Experiment had dashed the hopes of those who felt that measures short of production control would salvage the farmer.

Confused and appalled by the coexistence of rotting surpluses with widespread hunger and malnutrition, the nation's policymakers had three alternatives. They could keep hands off, as the dominant political forces had generally managed to do in the 1920's, and hope that divine economic laws would restore order and balance. They could regard an abundance of food as a unique national asset, and concentrate on its proper distribution, and on the restoration of the full employment which might lead to a natural absorption of the surpluses. Or they could slash farm production to correspond to the shrunken demand.

The first alternative was not a real one. The crisis was too severe and the stakes too great. Those favoring the second approach were only dimly aware of the degree to which farm surpluses reflected unemployment and low national income. Nor had they a well-thought-out program to give effect to their instincts. The last choice seemed the obvious one, at least to the farm organizations and the farm Congressmen. To be sure, it shied away from the massive fact that the real problems of agriculture in the early 1930's largely lay outside of agriculture.[10] But it was the logical outgrowth of our past thinking and experience, and it appeared to offer an immediate improvement in the condition of the farmers' market.

Industry had long followed the practice of trimming production to the level which demand would absorb—at a price profitable to the producer. Since the businessman was the pride and exemplar of the nation (especially during the 1920's) it was perhaps natural that agriculture should fall in step and plan in terms of a businessman's solution.

The Agricultural Adjustment Administration (AAA) of 1933, through which millions of farmers signed contracts to reduce acreage of surplus crops in return for direct federal payments, bowed before the Supreme Court early in 1936. To fill the void created by the Court's decision, the Soil Conservation and Domestic Allotment Act of 1936 was hastily put together. Since the crops plagued with chronic surpluses were also "soil-depleting" crops, the government agreed to pay farmers fixed sums per acre for growing "soil-building" crops and for not growing "soil-depleting" crops. This was intended to accomplish the threefold purpose of increasing farm income, promoting conservation needs, and reducing surpluses.

The severe drought of 1936 was followed by the record crops of 1937. Fresh surpluses drove farm prices sharply downward; and Congress, with an eye cocked on a Court rendered more pliable by President Roosevelt's "Court-packing" plan, responded with a comprehensive and far-reaching AAA program to curtail production and otherwise assist the hard-pressed farmer. The core of the AAA of 1938 was its implicit assumption that marketing and production controls should balance farm output with effective demand, rather than with potential demand, i.e., with known human needs. In creating this legislation, Congress assumed the need for a permanently managed agriculture to do battle with surpluses and boost farm income.

To meet the "surplus" problem head on, it prescribed a system of acreage allotments and marketing quotas for storable farm products. The latter were to become effective, however, only when surpluses above normal reserves had accumulated, and then only when approved by the vote of two-thirds of the producers affected.

The Commodity Credit Corporation (CCC), which stored the farmer's surplus "basic" commodities (wheat, corn, rice, tobacco, peanuts, and cotton) in good crop years and fed them back to the market in lean years, was given responsibility for managing the nation's "ever-normal granary." It operated through the newly created system of county AAA committee-men, chosen at local farmer elections to administer the AAA program. Using the storable commodities as collateral to be forfeited if not reclaimed by the individual farmers within a given marketing period—redemption was possible if farm prices rose above the loan level—the CCC was designed to help stabilize both farm prices and the nation's grain supply. The latter was of vital importance to the livestock industry, since the droughts of 1934 and 1936 had shown how seriously grain supply fluctuations affected the nation's supply and price of meat.

The act further provided for direct cash payments on basic commodities to co-operating farmers whenever production controls failed to bring farm income to "parity." Parity, as here defined, meant a farm income level derived from farm prices having the same purchasing power, per unit of product, as that enjoyed during the five favorable years immediately preceding the outbreak of World War I.

Having sheltered the farmers producing basic commodities from the rigors of the free market, Congress next established a limited system of crop insurance to protect individual farmers from the uncontrollable and unpredictable ravages of the weather itself. Producers of perishable commodities, accorded a kind of second-class status, were provided with a system of democratically controlled marketing agreements with which to regulate the nature and volume of their marketing flow. But no marketing quotas or cash benefits were available to them under the act.

The paradox of widespread malnutrition and artificially induced semi-scarcity continued to trouble many people. The New Deal atmosphere, stimulated by the continuing impact of the depression, gave rise to many earnest attempts to find a way to make surpluses serve human need. Experts pointed out that we would have to expand—not restrict—farm output if we were to provide our people with the food they really needed. The efforts of the under-consumptionists finally bore fruit in the school-lunch plan and the food-stamp plan. The latter set up a system for moving surplus foods, especially protective foods, through normal distribution channels to families on relief. The plan fell far short of meeting national nutritional needs, but it represented a notable step away from the scarcity approach of the AAA.

Several other agricultural programs should be mentioned in portraying the background picture of the Brannan Plan. The Rural Resettlement Administration (later renamed the Farm Security Administration and now called the Farmers' Home Administration) was established in 1935. It moved thousands of farmers from submarginal lands to family-sustaining soil. Whereas the AAA was oriented towards the larger commercial farmer, the Rural Resettlement Administration was concerned with bettering the living conditions and improving the economic opportunities of low-income farm families. It sought not merely to ameliorate their current poverty, but to help them attain higher living standards on a permanently self-sustaining basis.

Mortgage refinancing, production credit, rural electrification, and many lesser benisons also flowed from the legislative cornucopia of a farm-conscious Congress intent upon bringing "economic justice" to the farmer.

The droughts of the mid-1930's had aroused impressive popular support for the "ever-normal granary" system. It seemed to make good sense from the standpoint of both consumer and producer—a rare but happy combination. But it was not long before pressure from farm organizations and farm Congressmen began to warp the program. The AAA called for CCC loans at levels varying from 52 per cent to 75 per cent of parity, the precise level being left to the discretion of the Secretary of Agriculture. Demands for higher levels of support were soon heard, however, and Congress responded, after the passage of the Lend-Lease Act in 1941, by fixing supports first at 85 per cent and then at 90 per cent of parity.

From managing an ever-normal granary, the CCC was rapidly evolving into a price-jacking agency. The combination of high support levels, good crop years, and farmer resistance to CCC policies which *at any time* would lower farm prices, put a new and disturbing complexion on CCC activities. Since the movement of government-held grain into the market inevitably had a bearish effect on prices, the CCC was obliged to accumulate a volume of reserves that threatened to reach disabling proportions.

The Rome-Berlin-Tokyo Axis rescued the CCC, salvaging both its solvency and its prestige. Embarrassing reserves were magically transmuted by war into a vast and indispensable national resource. Food, said Secretary of Agriculture Wickard, would win the war and write the peace.

The "surplus" fixation was deeply entrenched in our pattern of thinking, however. Years of preoccupation with abundance, combined with the fright which CCC holdings had given the U.S. Department of Agriculture (USDA), provided the latter with an outlook that was hard to shake off. Despite the certainty that enormous amounts of food and fiber would be needed for ourselves and our Allies, it was 1944 before the Department finally removed all production controls.

During the war, the USDA operated not so much by regulation as by price inducement. The 90 per cent of parity price guarantee, made law in 1942, assured the farmer of sufficient price protection to encourage an all-out food and fiber production effort, and price guarantees above that level were used wherever the need was indicated. For example, we needed more flaxseed, more soybeans, and more peanuts, and needed them quickly. The USDA therefore gave advance guarantees of prices double that of the free market, and production of the needed crops soared.

The farmer enjoyed a period of extraordinary prosperity during World War II. Farm prices averaged from 106 per cent to 119 per cent of parity for the four war years, and net farm income increased from $5,300,000,000 in 1939 to $13,600,000,000 in 1944. In terms of purchasing power, farm income more than doubled during these years, partially because of good prices and partially because farm production increased at a phenomenal rate. Farm output rose to about 35 per cent above the 1935–39 level, despite the departure from the farms of some four and one-half million persons from 1940 to 1944.

The war and postwar consumption experience was regarded by some experts as a salutary reminder to the restrictionist school of the consumptive potentialities of a prosperous economy. Under conditions of full employment and good wages, domestic consumption of foods showed striking increases. Particularly in the area of milk, meat, and fresh fruits and vegetables, the American consumer abundantly vindicated the claims of the underconsumptionists.[11] The implications, as we shall see later, were not lost upon the USDA.

Congress had established contract termination and conversion policies which would cushion the impact of the peacetime readjustment period on industry. It was felt, therefore, that Congress owed a similar obligation to the farmer. Agriculture had made an incredible production record under the price guarantees and voracious markets of the wartime years, but substantial and painful readjustments were believed to lie ahead. Congress responded by enacting a statute to guarantee 90 per cent of parity for basic commodities for a period of two years following the official proclamation of war's end.

The same protection was extended by the Steagall Amendment to a number of perishable commodities for which substantial wartime increases in production had been asked. This amendment, passed by Congress at least partly to placate farmers for the imposition of wartime price ceilings on farm commodities, was expected to protect farm prices until the farmer could readjust his production pattern to postwar needs.

During the later war years and early postwar period an impressive amount of planning, both public and private, went into evolving a more satisfactory postwar agricultural policy. Many factors, some of them contradictory, were responsible for the increasing interest in agriculture. Millions of Americans were fearful that a major postwar depression was brewing and that only the most determined governmental efforts could keep the economy from collapsing. Many of these persons felt that national prosperity was peculiarly dependent on agricultural prosperity—or at least that agricultural price declines were the major precipitants of depression. Farmers were especially fearful that agriculture's burgeoning productive capacity would bring unprecedented postwar surpluses leading to disastrous price slumps.

On the other hand, there was a growing awareness among informed persons of the dependence of agriculture upon a full employment economy. The conviction was also developing that depression was preventable, and that relatively full employment had become a political imperative in America. Professional students of agriculture argued that the AAA of 1938 was better adapted to a depression economy than to the fully productive economy the nation seemed determined to have. Many of these students were also dissatisfied with price supports—particularly high-level price supports—as a means of achieving agricultural prosperity.

Some of the more significant studies on agricultural policy during this period, illustrating the extensiveness of interest in the subject, may be profitably cited. The titles, in some instances, are revealing. The Committee on Economic Development, a group of businessmen who look upon the federal government more as a partner than a foe, sponsored a special study published in 1943 entitled "Agriculture in an Expanding Economy." The National Planning Association issued several agricultural pamphlets including "For a Better Post-War Agriculture" (1942), "Dare Farmers Risk Abundance?" (1947), and "Must We Have Food Surpluses?" (1949).

The Association of Land-Grant Colleges and Universities, which as a settled practice shies delicately away from public policy matters lest it become tainted with partisanship, set up a committee which issued a report in 1944 entitled "Postwar Agricultural Policy." The association disclaimed responsibility for the views expressed, but it is noteworthy that it did encourage a substantive contribution to the discussion.[12]

The American Farm Economic Association sponsored a prize contest in February, 1945, for the best entries on the subject:

"A Price Policy for Agriculture, Consistent with Economic Progress, That Will Promote Adequate and More Stable Income from Farming." Over 300 entries were received and the prize-winning manuscripts (first prize, $5,000) were published.[13] The Association also established a committee of its own to study farm policy. Its report was one of the most important contributions to the growing agricultural literature of the period.[14]

Meanwhile, the USDA was busily spinning its own plans. The Department's "Interbureau Committee on Post-War Programs," established in 1941, did a substantial amount of research on postwar agricultural policy. In co-operation with the Bureau of Agricultural Economics (BAE), it prepared the testimony on postwar economic policies which was presented to Congress in August, 1944, by Secretary Claude Wickard.[15] The BAE issued a number of pamphlets which marshaled the relevant facts and trends in convenient form, suggested the questions which had to be answered, and in some instances sought to answer them.[16] These were published under the general heading, "What Peace Can Mean to American Farmers."

In April, 1945, a committee composed of personnel from the USDA and from the War Food Administration was created to study postwar agricultural policy. This committee issued no report, but it did prepare some useful working notes which were later used by the Policy and Program Committee when that body was handed the planning functions formerly assigned to BAE.

The Policy and Program Committee, organized on January 1, 1946, began major planning operations on December 30, 1946. Secretary of Agriculture Clinton Anderson detailed Assistant Secretary Brannan to head the subcommittee on long-range planning. This subcommittee, utilizing the planning studies instituted by former Secretary Claude Wickard, did intensive work for nearly a year in drawing up the testimony presented to the Senate and House agricultural committees in 1947.[17]

Congress also felt the urge to plan. During the war the House of Representatives established a Special Committee on Postwar

Economic Policy and Planning, which held a number of hearings on postwar agricultural policy, and issued a report entitled *Postwar Economic Policy and Planning (Summary and Conclusions)*.[18]

In 1947, conscious of the ten-year lapse since the last really comprehensive legislative review of national agricultural policy, the House and Senate agricultural committees girded themselves for a major effort. The House Committee held hearings in Washington from April 21, 1947 to July 17, 1947. Then, in an attempt to directly tap "grass-roots" sentiment, both House and Senate agricultural committees packed their bags and held field hearings throughout the nation—a legislative experiment without precedent in the agricultural field. Again in 1948 lengthy hearings preceded and accompanied the formulation of the Hope-Aiken Act.

All in all, the nation had witnessed one of the most intensive and thoroughgoing reviews of a major legislative problem in recent decades.

Out of this agricultural ferment emerged the Agricultural Act of 1948, which eventually came to be regarded as the Republican Party's contribution to the welfare of the American farmer. This act, however, far from offering the nation a program representing unified Republican thinking, emphasized the sharp and fundamental differences which had been developing within agriculture and within each of the major parties.

Title I (Republican Representative Clifford Hope's bill) of the Agricultural Act of 1948 continued inflexible 90 per cent of parity price supports for another year, while Title II (Republican Senator George Aiken's bill) prescribed a system of flexible price supports, to become effective January 1, 1950, with a lower and upper limit of 60 per cent and 90 per cent of parity, the existing level to be proportioned to the supply. A 72 per cent to 90 per cent parity guarantee was authorized when marketing quotas or acreage allotments were in effect.

Congressman Hope's bill enjoyed solid backing from the South and also from a considerable number of northern representatives from each party. The Aiken Bill, on the other hand, commanded bipartisan support in the Senate, only three Senators recording their opposition to it.

Although the Hope section was generally regarded as transitional legislation, with Aiken's contribution to become permanent national policy after 1949, the precariousness of Senator Aiken's contribution was apparent from the first to close students of agricultural politics. Both House and Senate conference committee members, when attempting to reconcile the differences between the Senate and House bills, were adamant in defending their parity views. The cotton and tobacco growers—no lovers of flexible parity—had well-entrenched spokesmen in the House Committee on Agriculture, and they had no intention of yielding to the Senate any further than was absolutely necessary.

Since all price support legislation was expiring this very day (and because GOP members of Congress wanted to adjourn so they could attend the Republican convention at Philadelphia the next day) a shot-gun wedding of the Hope-Aiken bills appeared to be the only way out of the dilemma.

The wedding was consummated accordingly, but only after House conferees made it clear that they were not conceding ultimate victory to the Aiken-led forces. The adjournment period was accepted on both sides as no more than a breather between rounds.

The Aiken flexible price support formula, approved in substance by all of the major farm organizations, was formally endorsed by the platforms of both political parties in the 1948 conventions. President Truman's criticism of Republican farm policy during the 1948 campaign was not directed at the flexible provisions of the Aiken Bill, to which he had formally extended his blessing. On October 12, 1948, for example, Mr. Truman told a campaign audience that "we must have on a permanent basis a system of flexible price supports for agricultural commodities." [19] His wrath was centered primarily upon the proviso in the Commodity Credit Corporation Charter Act which clipped the storage wings of the CCC,[20] and upon the alleged determination of the Republicans to weaken or destroy the entire price support system.

Lesser Democrats, on the other hand, were busy in some areas spreading the word that 60 per cent of parity was mighty thin gruel for the hard days ahead. Various charges have been made that the Production and Marketing Administration (PMA) committeemen were also engaged in sowing these warnings,[21] although these charges seem not to have been verified.

The Democrats rode back to power in November, 1948. Brannan, who had accepted the secretaryship at a time when most persons regarded it as a dead-end road, was now enjoying the prestige which his intelligence, administrative ability, and successful campaigning had won him. The Democrats were in the mood to get farm legislation on the books freed from the taint of the "do-nothing, good-for-nothing" 80th Congress and Secretary Brannan was willing to do his part.

Meanwhile, several economic developments were forcing the issue. The USDA's obligation to support the price of certain perishable commodities at relatively high levels until December 31, 1949, was brewing a pot of trouble. The government was buying millions of dozens of eggs and storing them in a cave in Kansas. Price-support operations on potatoes were going to cost over $100,000,000 for the fiscal year of 1948–49. The nation had been scandalized by the outright destruction of potatoes, and was only partially mollified by the frantic attempts to use government-purchased potatoes for inefficient diversionary purposes.

Powdered milk was accumulating in large quantities and threatened to create an undisposable reserve. It began to look as if the government might have to buy hogs and store pork at a time when consumers were already complaining about meat prices. The Steagall amendment, providing price support for many perishables, was due to expire on December 31, 1949. Some kind of substitute legislation was called for, unless the producers of perishables were to be left to the mercies of a free market.

Meanwhile, the prosperity of the immediate postwar years

was beginning to recede. Farm income dropped 15 per cent in 1948. A further drop of 10 to 15 per cent was anticipated for 1949. Fears of depression, with the farmers bearing the initial and heaviest shock, were spreading. Grain surpluses impended, and the first wheat acreage allotments in many years appeared to be just ahead.

This, then, was the setting for the Brannan Plan. The supporters of Hope's rigid price-support formula and of Aiken's flexible price-support plan were squaring away for a return bout. The triumphant Democrats were feeling their oats, and were ill-disposed to let major agricultural legislation bear an "80th Congress" label. Perishables were in trouble. Farm prices and farm income were slipping rapidly. And an ambitious and capable Secretary of Agriculture had shed the inhibitions of a shaky short-term appointment.

ORIGIN

Where did the Brannan Plan come from? The question has intrigued many, and some fascinating answers have been given. For example:

"The Brannan Plan was first specifically outlined in the resolutions adopted in the national convention of the CIO at Portland, Oregon, last November." [22]

"Most of the recommendations of the Secretary appear to be simply the provisions of the Agriculture Act of 1948 in a new dress." [23]

"Mr. Speaker, Members of Congress have learned from an authoritative source that the much publicized Brannan farm plan is the brain child of Henry Wallace, Rexford Tugwell and Alger Hiss. Prepared when Wallace was Secretary of Agriculture, when both Tugwell and Hiss worked for Wallace, it was buried for several years in the musty archives of the D.A. and then resurrected by Mr. Brannan when he became Secretary." [24]

"The Secretary should have no trouble in completely formulating his plans. His whole scheme . . . is bodily lifted from the Italian Plan in use just before the outbreak of World War II." [25]

"The nominal author of this bill is Secretary of Agriculture Brannan. Its spiritual author is James G. Patton, head of the National Farmers Union." [26]

"Secretary Brannan's plan is his own." [27]

These represent a fair sample of the conjectures which have been advanced concerning the genesis of the Brannan Plan. Now for a look at the evidence.

Any study of policy formulation must include not only the over-all economic and social factors which predispose decision-making in a certain way, but also the background, characteristics, and convictions of the central personalities involved. If major historical events are largely the surface manifestations of powerful, impersonal undercurrents shaping the broad outlines of social developments, it can hardly be denied that individual men of force and capacity not only influence the undercurrents, but also select between the range of alternatives which are possible in a given historical context. History is the story not only of forces, but of conflicting or divergent forces working amidst men with conflicting or divergent ideas, interests, desires, hopes and fears. By lending their weight to this force rather than that, and by appealing to this popular desire rather than that, historical figures materially influence the course of history.

Charles Franklin Brannan was born in 1903 at Denver, Colorado. He worked his way through Regis College in Denver, transferred to Denver University where he was elected president of the student body, and served as law librarian while attending Denver University Law School. After passing the bar at the age of twenty-six, he began the practice of law, which sometimes provided slim pickings during the lean days of the Great Depression.

In 1935 he was appointed Assistant Regional Attorney in the Resettlement Administration. His job was to interview destitute farmers in the "dust bowl," and to arrange for the resettlement of farmers from that tragic area. During the course of his two-year association with the Resettlement Administration, he purchased approximately a million acres of waste land and supervised the movement of its occupants to more productive land. In the course of these poignant experiences, Brannan almost inevitably acquired a sense of the overriding importance of conservation.

For the next four years, Brannan served as Regional Attorney in the Department of Agriculture's Office of the Solicitor. Moving over into the office of Regional Director of the Farm Security Administration in 1941, he spent two and one-half years administering loans for water facilities and handling credit arrangements for needy families in Colorado, Wyoming, and Montana.

Brannan's experiences with the Farm Security Administration made a deep impression on him. A devoted New Dealer from the early days of Mr. Roosevelt's administration, and a man described by his friends as possessing a keen sense of social justice, Brannan's work with the Farm Security Administration developed or confirmed several important convictions. First, he acquired a special interest in the welfare of low-income farmers—particularly those entangled in unfortunate social and economic circumstances largely beyond their control. Second, he began to conceive of government as specially obligated, if necessary by means of a centrally planned program, to help promote the ultimate independence and self-reliance of these farmers. In brief, Brannan was moved by the same generous, humanitarian impulses which marked the zeal and crusading fervor of so many Americans during the exciting days of the early and mid-1930's. Like his fellow liberals, he conceived of government as an active instrument for democratically achieving the liberation of trapped men and women, for bringing them from the ragged fringes of society into its central warmth and fruitfulness. Government was viewed as an instrument of immensely fertile potentialities.

Brannan's energy and efficiency attracted the attention of his superiors, and he was called to Washington in 1944 to be Assistant Administrator of the Farm Security Administration. The quality of his work in connection with war problems led to his appointment, during the same year, as Assistant Secretary of Agriculture under Claude Wickard.

In Washington, Brannan moved in a circle of New Deal liberals. With none, however, was he more intimate than with Jim Patton, the forceful, persuasive, and shrewd farm leader who became president of the National Farmers Union in 1940. The two had been good friends in Colorado for many years, and were particularly close during the days when Brannan was Regional Director of the Farm Security Administration in Denver and Patton was working for the Farmers Union in the same area. Somewhat later, Patton is reported to have worked hard to get Brannan appointed as Assistant Secretary of Agriculture (June, 1944), and as Secretary of Agriculture (May, 1948).[28]

Mr. Patton was one of the more ardent New Dealers. He was an unabashed believer in national planning, in positive government (especially when used on behalf of underprivileged elements), in the general beneficence of labor unions and in their underlying harmony of interest with farmers. He was an outspoken foe of business monopoly, a defender of civil liberties for heretics, and a full-blown internationalist. He played an important part in shaping the Full Employment Act of 1946. That Mr. Patton was a man with a fully matured body of well-integrated philosophical and political concepts was conceded by his bitterest enemies—of whom he had and has many.

After the war ended, Brannan entered upon a period of relative inactivity galling to one of his temperament and ambition. Senator Clinton P. Anderson (D–N. Mex., then Secretary of Agriculture) stated that his personal secretary called his attention to Brannan's restlessness. Brannan was contemplating accepting an appointment to the Indian Claims Commission, although he had little enthusiasm for the job. Anderson promptly gave Brannan the job of managing the subcommittee on long-range planning of the Policy and Program Committee.[29]

Brannan's friends suggest that Anderson's decision was precipitated by a verbal exchange with Brannan. According to them, Secretary Anderson launched the Department's long-range planning program with the suggestion that "we should attempt to determine how much farm output can be profitably produced." Brannan countered with the observation that this was putting the cart before the horse. The departmental policy, he said, should be directed towards a production goal geared to what the people needed, not merely to what could be profitably produced. All right, the Secretary allegedly said, if that is your approach, how about heading up the long-range planning group and see what you can work out?

The Assistant Secretary worked hard in his new assignment. When the House called upon Anderson to testify in April, 1947, Brannan had prepared a document which pulled together the thinking of all the leading departmental figures, and represented what administrators are fond of referring to as an "organizational product."

Brannan's appointment as Secretary of Agriculture, following Anderson's resignation to run on the Democratic ticket as Senator from New Mexico, raised only a slight ripple in the political pond. The *New York Times* reported: "When President Truman named Charles F. Brannan Secretary of Agriculture late in May, 1948, the most generous reaction was that Mr. Truman had given the Government career service another nice shot in the arm. A man who had served the Department faithfully for thirteen years and who had climbed the ladder from a $3700 a year farm resettlement attorney in Denver had earned a fitting reward in Washington." [30]

Brannan's tenure as Secretary of Agriculture in 1948 was largely uneventful except for his vigorous campaigning on behalf of Mr. Truman's candidacy.

Then, soon after his appointment Harold Stassen, intending to help his erstwhile rival, Thomas E. Dewey, along to the Presidency, accused the Department of Agriculture of using farm price supports to hold up food prices until after the election. Brannan, burning at charges against his favorite Government agency, hit the campaign trail.[31] Some dozen weeks and eighty speeches later a great many people had learned to recognize not only the name but also the man. What the public saw and heard is generally conceded, even by Republicans, to have persuaded numbers of voters to keep President Truman in office. It also convinced Mr. Truman that he had in the serious Brannan, if hardly a White House crony, certainly an able lieutenant.[32]

Some of the public statements made by the Secretary prior to April 7, 1949 will throw light on the controversial question of whether the Brannan Plan was a natural outgrowth of previously held convictions, or a departure from some of the views he had held earlier.

Speaking at the Catholic Tri-State Congress on September 17, 1947, Brannan was reported as saying that the family farm is the "cornerstone of our national strength" and "one of the most effective bulwarks any nation can have against Communism."

At Bridgeton, New Jersey, September 26, 1948, the Secretary "declared . . . that farmers must fight to preserve their farm programs but urged also that farm prices be correlated to the ability of the consumer to pay."

On October 19, 1948, he was quoted as advocating "a national program of long-range and permanent agricultural abundance, in contrast to the prewar programs of creating artificial scarcities." Brannan's views on this subject may have grown out of his experience with Farm Security Administration. Officials of this agency, having firsthand evidence of rural malnutrition, were never sympathetic with the AAA approach of production control.

Shortly after the election Brannan said: "We can't get real parity merely by jockeying price support levels. We must relate our soil conservation and crop insurance to price support." [33] He indicated that shifts in type of agriculture would prove more satisfactory in avoiding surplus production than would legislative restriction. "Increased meat consumption in this country would point to a shift of some of our grain land to a grass and livestock economy," he said. "And that would be good soil conservation practice." [34]

Speaking at the annual meeting of the Farmers Union Grain Terminal Association at St. Paul, Minnesota, on December 14, 1948, Brannan announced: "I shall fight with all my strength any notion that the farmer must lead the way to a lower scale of purchasing power or a lower scale of living. Parity is more than an objective—more than a nice ideal—more than a matter of justice. It is an economic imperative. Parity is essential to the general welfare." [35]

Where did Brannan stand on the question of flexible price supports prior to 1949? The following exchange which took place before the House Committee on Agriculture on April 11, 1949, points up an interesting facet of the question.

Mr. Hoeven (Representative from Iowa): "Is it not a fact that the Administration has proposed, and you have proposed, flexible price supports on a permanent basis at the time the Aiken bill was enacted?"

Mr. Brannan: "Mr. Hoeven, may I respectfully say to you that that has been charged a number of times. Mr. Taft confronted me with it one day on a radio program. I have asked him to produce the evidence that caused him to think we had." [36]

This was a touchy subject with the Secretary and he repeatedly denied that he had ever committed himself to flexible price supports. At one stage he wrote Senator Thomas, chairman of the Senate Committee on Agriculture and Forestry, pointing out that the word "flexible" in connection with price programs, had been widely construed to mean the sliding scale, whereas he contended it had a much broader meaning than that.[37] He sought to leave the impression, without flatly coming out and saying so, that "flexibility" as he had conceived it, meant no more than a variety of administrative choices in dealing with agricultural problems.

The following evidence would have proved useful to Senator Taft. Secretary Brannan was in charge of the long-range agricultural planning program which drew up the Department's recommendations to Congress in 1947. This program, among other things, stated that "a high degree of flexibility, both as to support levels and methods, is essential in view of differences between commodities and constantly changing conditions that cannot be foreseen." [38]

It could be argued that this was not conclusive evidence, since Carl Farrington of the Production and Marketing Administration was in charge of the study group drawing up this section of the departmental testimony. However, Senator Anderson asserts that Brannan at no time during the development of the long-range testimony expressed dissatisfaction with the idea of flexible price supports.[39] He also stated that Brannan had "the full responsibility" for evolving the long-range program offered by the Department.[40]

The *New York Times,* upon Brannan's assumption of the secretaryship, reported: "Mr. Brannan told an informal news conference today that he planned to follow the policies of former Secretary Anderson. 'I am a great admirer of Anderson,' he said. 'He did a wonderful job as Secretary. I think it is best to keep his program going.' He stated that he was vitally interested in obtaining Congressional approval of the long-range farm program *with a system of flexible farm price supports.*" [41] (Italics mine.)

Then, on June 25, 1948, in response to a request from the Budget Bureau for its views on the Hope-Aiken Act, Brannan wrote to Director James E. Webb as follows: "There are several provisions which we consider objectionable. We object to the provisions which give special treatment to certain commodities such as those which virtually assure a mandatory price support of 90 per cent of parity for tobacco and wool for at least several years. We object, even though the provisions apply only to 1949, to the mandatory 90 per cent of parity or comparable price for hogs, chickens, eggs, and milk and its products . . . Notwithstanding these objections, we recommend that the President approve the bill."

On July 4, 1948, President Truman, acting in accordance with Brannan's recommendations, declared: "The Agricultural Act which was signed today . . . does not provide the basic declaration of long-range agricultural policy which is needed to round out the present farm program. Instead, the Congress had to act at the last moment to prevent the death of certain existing programs and found only enough time to make a gesture toward long-range policy. The portions of the bill which approach long-range planning do not go into effect until 1950." [42]

The long-range policy, it should be re-emphasized, contained flexible price supports as its keystone, and the President's complaint about the Hope-Aiken Act was that flexible price supports were postponed until 1950 instead of being put into effect immediately.

When the above statements are combined with Brannan's failure to recommend repeal of the "sliding scale" at any time during the 1948 campaign, the evidence is clear that Brannan, whether out of expediency or conviction, did approve flexible price supports prior to the election of 1948.

Early in January, 1949, the chairmen of the House and Senate agriculture committees phoned Brannan to ask that he prepare testimony for early submission before their committees. The Secretary put in a call for O. V. Wells, the lucid and knowledgeable head of the Bureau of Agricultural Economics. He asked Wells to chair a departmental seminar on national agricultural policy, to organize the agenda, and generally bring out the vital current facts, trends, and problems involved. He wanted, said the Secretary, to get a thorough briefing himself, and he wanted to sound out departmental thinking at the same time.

Approximately twenty departmental officers were detailed to attend regularly the seminar sessions which Mr. Wells now began to organize. Another eighteen or twenty men, most of them specialists in the particular areas under discussion at a given seminar session, were called in at one time or another to participate. The regular members included the Secretary; his Executive Assistant, Wesley McCune; Undersecretary Albert Loveland and his assistant, William Chandler; Louis Bean, the well-known economist and opinion analyst; Nathan Koenig, Executive Assistant under former Secretary Clinton P. Anderson; Philip F. Aylesworth, Secretary of the Policy and Program Committee; John Baker, drawn from the Fats and Oil branch of PMA for this particular assignment; the Solicitor, W. Carroll Hunter, and Assistant Solicitor, Edward Shulman; the Director of Information, Keith Himebaugh and his assistant, Maurice DuMars; O. V. Wells and two assistants from BAE, O. C. Stine and Karl Fox; Claude Wickard, former Secretary of Agriculture who moved over to become Administrator of Rural Electrification Administration; Ralph S. Trigg, Administrator of PMA, his Deputy Administrator, Frank Woolley, and Gus Geissler, then manager of F.C.I.C. and later Administrator of PMA; and Lionel Holm, Elmer Kruse, J. Murray Thompson, Don Stoops, and John I. Thompson, also from PMA.[43]

The first of eight seminars assembled January 26, 1949, with subsequent meetings continuing for several hours twice a week (with two exceptions) until March 3. The Secretary gave Mr. Wells a completely free hand in organizing and managing the seminar. Prior to several of the meetings, working notes were prepared by a member of the Department expert in the subject to be discussed. These notes, distributed in advance of the meetings, presented pertinent background and/or factual material, and posed some of the leading questions. Either Mr. Wells, or someone designated by him, led out in the discussions, with all members free to participate in the general discussion which followed. Participants were invited to contribute their own ideas as well as to comment on those brought forward by the discussion leader.

Brannan said little until the sixth meeting. He knew that if he were to tip his hand on how his thinking was running it would dry up or deflect the contributions of the more timid— or more ambitious—members. As it was, some members were reported to be industriously attempting to anticipate the Secretary, and project into the discussions their interpretations of such rather vague policy statements as the Secretary was known to have made in the past. This development, of course, was inevitable in an assemblage of twenty leading departmental figures.

The subject matter for the seminars included the Agricultural Act of 1948, recommendations of leading farm experts and of the major farm organizations, problems of supporting perishable commodities, compensatory payments, multiple-price systems, income parity as an alternative to price parity, the food-stamp plans, and modernization of parity. During these discussions nearly all of the more important ideas current in agricultural circles came in for some attention.

Probably no subject was more fully explored than compensatory payments, that is, the use of direct federal payments as a substitute for price supports. Practically all prominent agricultural economists were favorably disposed to this method—as we shall note later on—and the seminar would have been badly out of step with the times had it failed to give attention to them.

A paper on compensatory payments was prepared in the Bureau of Agricultural Economics for advance distribution to seminar members. It contained a number of statements which are worth noting:

Cost to government will generally be higher with compensatory payments than with price supports. . . . Money savings to consumers under compensatory payments will usually equal or exceed the amount of the payments themselves. . . . Total domestic consumption would be less with price supports than under compensatory payments. . . . Price support programs are limited by *availability of acceptable diversion outlets.* . . . If support purchases . . . exceed available food outlets, it might be preferable to use compensatory payments even though the direct cost to Government would be somewhat higher. . . . Administrative problems involved would not be insurmountable . . . it is frequently said that farmers are hostile to compensatory payments because they involve accepting a Government check or "subsidy." However, if the guaranteed farm return is a fixed point of public policy, it is really the consumer who is being subsidized by the compensatory payment. If the Government check is distasteful to farmers, it might be paid to certified dealers or processors who have paid farmers the full guaranteed return. It seems likely that this attitude toward Government checks could be overcome wherever compensatory payments could be shown to have clearcut advantages to the general public . . . in conclusion, it seems likely that compensatory payments would be preferable to price supports on some livestock products *if extensive operations were required.* Small surpluses might be handled more readily through price support and diversion. On storable commodities such as feed grains which are mainly for domestic consumption, price support and storage seem generally preferable . . . In the case of potatoes, compensatory payments would cost the Government a great deal more than price supports.

During the seminar meetings, no effort was made to arrive at a consensus of thinking, nor could it be said that a consensus naturally emerged from the discussion, except on a few points. As Mr. Wells put it, the seminars brought the leading questions in agricultural policy out in the open; they were not designed to answer them. The alternatives were laid bare, but even tentative decision-making was avoided. One highly significant piece of evidence suggests, however, that decision-making was already well on its way before the seminars ended, although the members themselves were either unaware or only dimly aware of the fact.

On the evening of the sixth meeting, the Secretary bestirred himself to mark out some of the guideposts which he thought sound farm policy should steer by. Although notes are skimpy and memories vague on much of what took place in the seminar session, Philip F. Aylesworth, Secretary of the Program and Planning Committee, took down a fairly complete outline of the Secretary's remarks, and reproduced them in a memorandum to Wells on the next day. The following is quoted from Aylesworth's memorandum:

C. General criteria
    d) Relate supply to genuine demand (not demand conditioned by price).
D. Major points.
    1. Parity formula.
        a) Develop some new way of establishing parity (to express equity, so the objective can be 100 per cent.
        b) Price supports are only a means to an end. Objective is parity income . . .
        c) Reasonable relationship of farm income to national income.
        d) Take steps—four to five years—to get to genuine parity (equity).

3. Application of programs.
    a) Compensatory payments for some commodities.
    b) Distinction between aids for perishables and nonperishables.
    g) How related to . . . conservation.
    h) Interest of city people.
4. Good income of farm people essential to labor and industry.
6. Proposals should be equally acceptable by any audience—apartment dweller or farmer.
7. Consider graduating price supports down by volume of production (size of farm). There is danger in following the will-o-the-wisp of increased efficiency of industrial type farms.[44]

Here, unmistakably, is the heart of the Brannan Plan. Here is the concept of income parity expressed in terms of 100 per cent of parity price supports, of compensatory payments (implying a free market) for some commodities, of a distinction between perishables and storables, of a program related to conservation needs, of a limitation on benefits available to factory-type farms, and of a program with consumer as well as producer appeal. The mechanics may not have been clearly fixed in the Secretary's mind, but there can be no doubt that he already knew in which direction he was going.[45]

There was considerable disappointment among some members when the Secretary arose, on the evening of the last meeting, March 3, to thank the participants for their presence and for their help. He added that the seminar was too large to do the work which lay ahead, and that he would have to call upon a smaller group to work out the policies which the Department would recommend and the testimony which would be presented to Congress.

Shortly thereafter the Secretary called five men into his office. They were Wesley McCune, O. V. Wells, Ralph S. Trigg, John Baker, and Maurice DuMars. McCune, a long-time student of agricultural policy and a writer of distinction,[46] was an obvious selection because of his position. DuMars was chosen because of his professional writing experience with the Department. Wells was included because his agency, the BAE, had the facts, and because his judgment and knowledge were respected by all of his associates. Trigg was a natural choice, as the administrator of the most powerful agency in the Department—PMA—and as the man who would have to make a price program work. Baker, possessing a substantial background of professional training and administrative experience in federal agricultural programs, was brought in as a general assistant and as a liaison man between the working group and such technical experts as might have to be called upon during the coming weeks.[47]

The following narration of the Secretary's remarks does not purport to be verbally precise. It does, however, represent the substance of his observations [48] as the six men settled down to work.

The major questions agricultural policy must settle upon, as Brannan explained it to his five assistants, appeared to be these:

1. Should farm prices be supported at high, medium, or low levels?
2. Which commodities should be supported?
3. How shall the various commodities be supported, especially perishables?
4. What limitations or conditions should attach to the granting of support?

"Do we agree that these are crucial points?" Brannan asked. The working group did. "We have a choice," the Secretary continued, "between medium, low, or high price supports. I choose high. The problem will be to determine how high and by what formula we arrive at our level." The Secretary then proceeded approximately as follows:

I am very much interested in moving over from a parity price support standard to an income support standard since income, after all, is what counts. Prices are only a means to an end, that end being income. If we can work it out, I would like to establish an income support goal by which our price supports can be gauged. I would like an income standard which will assure the farmer a reasonably fair share of the national income, and set up price supports at 100 per cent of that goal. If the standard is equitable, I see no valid reason for talking about 60 per cent of equity or 72 per cent or 90 per cent. Let's be done with fractional justice and aim for the real thing.

Furthermore, I think the evidence shows that flexible price supports do not bring about the production adjustments its proponents claim.

Another thing. I see no justification for supporting the price of a few commodities, and leaving the bulk of farm produce with little or no protection. I am interested in working out a method for giving equal support to as many commodities as possible, and especially to those which contribute most to the national income. If we are going to keep farm prices from skidding further and pulling the nation down into a serious depression, we will have to support more than storable commodities alone. Finally, I want to tie our program into the soil conservation picture and into the needs of the family farm. I have no desire to further the interests of assembly-line farming. In the past, promoting the interests of family farms has been like the weather—everybody talks about it but nobody does anything. I would like to really do something about it.

With these prefatory comments, the working group commenced the exacting and arduous work which was required to hammer out the details and select the techniques for reaching the Secretary's predetermined ends.

It would be erroneous to assume that Brannan and his assistants drove straight ahead, without any false steps, towards the proposals which were later dubbed the Brannan Plan. Although the major elements of the Plan were in the works from the start, intensive work was done on several proposals which were later discarded.

The decision which established an income standard of support convertible into price supports at high levels is of special interest. When the arguments against the Brannan Plan are boiled down, and the emotional froth is skimmed away, most of the rational opposition to the Plan derived from what critics regarded as an excessively high standard of support. (This objection will be analyzed in the following chapter.) It has already been pointed out that Brannan, at the beginning of the "cabinet" meetings, "chose" high price supports. The decision was strictly his, and represented his recently acquired view that this was in the best interests of agriculture (and possibly in the best interests of the Democratic party as well).

It seems certain that one key statistic had made a tremendous impression on Brannan's thinking. Per capita farm income was only 60 per cent of per capita nonfarm income! That fact apparently revolved around and around in his mind and deeply colored his thinking on price supports. With farm income at this appallingly low level, how could he justify either moderate or flexible price supports, neither of which could be relied upon to alter this massive inequity?

The Secretary, then, had made up his mind to recommend high price supports. He also resolved to move from price supports with a 1909–14 base to supports related to some kind of up-to-date farm income goal. The Aiken Act had provided him with a convenient excuse by virtually instructing the Department to work out an income parity standard. Furthermore, it was obvious to him that the income parity used under the AAA of 1938 was no longer of value. Under its calculations the farmers were making 60 per cent more than they deserved, while his central statistical thesis demonstrated that they were getting 40 per cent less than he thought was rightfully theirs.

The Secretary, as mentioned before, had already stated his preference for a support formula which could be applied as 100 per cent. It would be both politically dangerous and contrary to his objectives if he were to come up with an income parity formula which reduced current support guarantees, and then sought to disguise the fact by calling them 100 per cent of a new standard.

The Farmers Union had just gone on record endorsing 100 per cent of parity price supports. A probable majority of the members of Congress were ready to stand by 90 per cent of parity, and the Secretary was personally certain that the American farmer wanted no less. If he were to recommend "high" price supports, it followed that the formula would have to produce support levels as high as 90 per cent of parity, and possibly somewhere between 90 per cent and 100 per cent.

The Secretary turned over the thorny job of working out a formula to Wells and BAE, hopeful that they could devise an income standard which would plausibly meet the specifications in which he was interested. During the course of this particular piece of research, Brannan's preoccupation with farm and non-farm income differentials led him back to an idea he had expressed during the sixth seminar session. Would it be possible, he asked Wells, to come up with a formula which was not so high initially as to be unacceptable, but which would gradually push support levels up and thereby close at least part of the income gap? [49]

Aiken's Title II had legislatively introduced the idea of a ten year moving average, to be used in the price-support formula in adjusting prices *within* agriculture, but which did not affect the total over-all relationship between farm and nonfarm prices. BAE discovered that the ten year moving average concept could be admirably adapted to the Secretary's objectives.

The income support standard finally worked out was based on the assumption that the purchasing power enjoyed by farmers from 1939 to 1948 should be maintained. Dividing total cash farm receipts from 1939 to 1948 by the index of prices paid for goods during those years gave farmers an average purchasing power of slightly over $18 billion during this base period. To compute the farm income goal for 1950, then, it was only necessary to discover how many dollars farmers should receive from cash receipts at 1950 price levels to match farm purchasing power in 1939–48.

Since prices were expected to be 44 per cent higher in 1950 than during the base period, multiplying $18 billion by 44 per cent gave an income goal of approximately $26 billion. To determine the price or income support for a particular commodity, the average price of that commodity during the base period would be increased sufficiently to give it a purchasing power equivalent to that which it enjoyed during the base period.

The standard met a number of the Secretary's preferred criteria.

1. It included the war and immediate postwar years, the period in which farmers—at least most of them—flourished as never before. Farm purchasing power during this period, therefore, could be conveniently translated into an income support standard which reflected the Secretary's yearning for guaranteed high-level farm income.

2. Translated into specific price supports for individual commodities, support levels resulted which closely approximated the modernized parity levels in Aiken's Title II. This would help allay suspicion about the new formula, and make the transition from a price base to an income base more acceptable.

3. Like the Aiken modernized parity, the income standard would be reflected in more favorable returns for producers of meat and dairy products, as contrasted with producers of basic commodities.

4. Using the first ten of the last twelve years, a device which would give the agricultural statisticians an opportunity to appraise fully farm pricing developments, the formula would insure a gradual rise in price support levels. To illustrate, the years to be used in computing the initial price support standard would be 1938–47, since Brannan would be proposing his Plan in 1949. However, as the low income years of 1938, 1939, and 1940 were sloughed off one by one, they would be replaced with the high income years of 1948, 1949, and 1950, thereby fattening price and income support levels. The increase might amount to a substantial increment of 5 to 6 per cent, and would be increased still further because of the steady exodus of farmers to the city. This would mean that the relatively fixed income goal would be divided annually among about 100,000 fewer farms.

Meanwhile, other work was going forward. In line with his basic philosophy, Secretary Brannan wanted production geared to need, rather than to effective demand. How could this be best accomplished? To begin with, Brannan construed our wartime experiences as proof that high support levels promote abundant production. Since he wanted abundant production, the income support standard he was seeking would contribute importantly to that end. But some way must be found to guarantee that our abundance would be consumed instead of swelling our supplies of surplus stocks.

Two main alternatives presented themselves. Consumption could be directly stimulated via some kind of food-stamp plan, possibly supplemented by an expanded school lunch program. Or price supports could be jettisoned for at least some crops, and replaced by a system of compensatory payments. In this case, farm products for which additional consumption was desired would find their natural level in a free market, and the farmer would be subsidized sufficiently to net him a return that would encourage continued maximum production.

The food-stamp plan of 1939 was hardly appropriate for postwar conditions, since it involved the movement of surplus foods to persons on relief. Relief rolls were not large, and the Secretary did not want to base his Plan on an anticipation that they would become so. His Plan was designed to *prevent* depression, not to deal with it. Senator Aiken, however, had presented a food-stamp proposal which was more adaptable to postwar conditions. Aiken's plan would permit anyone to buy food stamps, but families would have to turn over 40 per cent of their income to the government in return for their weekly quota of stamps (valued at five dollars per person). This requirement would make it unprofitable for any but low-income families to purchase stamps.

The Secretary and his assistants studied this plan, discussed it fully and somewhat sympathetically, but finally concluded that it was less adequate for the Secretary's purposes than the alternative of direct payments. Per public dollar expended, more direct benefits were believed to accrue to the consuming public through a compensatory payment program than from a food-stamp plan.

The decision to substitute direct payments for price supports in the field of perishables was thoroughly consistent with the Secretary's philosophy and with the total economic setting. As mentioned above, he wanted as many commodities protected as possible. The Department, acting under Congressional order, had already run into trouble and suffered severe (if unfair) criticism through its potato purchase program. It naturally wanted to avoid identification with a program which was certain to antagonize the general public and provide its enemies with ready-made ammunition.

Potatoes were not the only problem, as indicated before. The egg storage program was promising plenty of headaches, with the end nowhere in sight. Hog purchases were becoming a distinct probability. With farm prices dropping steadily, there appeared to be no prospect of disposing of the growing stockpile of foodstuffs in ways that would serve the public interest. Apparently the only alternatives to compensatory payments were to continue withdrawing from the market food which the Secretary wanted consumed—with the possibility of eventual food spoilage or outright destruction—or to drop price support levels to prevent excessive accumulation. The latter was equally unacceptable, since Brannan was interested in a program which would sustain farm income at what he regarded as a fair level, encourage continued production, and buttress the economy of the whole nation.

Another factor contributed heavily to the decision to recommend production payments. Brannan was an ardent "underconsumptionist" with an awareness of the nutritional deficiencies of the national consumption pattern. People wanted more meat and milk. Given an opportunity, they would gladly consume more, as the recent war had shown. Now if farmers were given the incentive of high support levels on livestock, if the increased production which this would presumably bring were reflected to the consumer in lower prices, and if the livestock farmer's income were maintained by direct payments instead of price supports—thereby making possible the potential consumer advantages—then a variety of desirable ends would be served. More animals would consume more grain, thus disposing of potential surpluses. If grain surpluses were consumed, the necessity for acreage controls and marketing quotas would be greatly reduced —a development which would be welcomed by farmers, economists, and those who feared "Big Government." More livestock would also require most pasture land and more leguminous production, which would be a boon to the cause of conservation. Finally, this step would make possible expanded consumption of the very foods nutritionists were saying we needed.

It was an attractive package for someone with the Secretary's predilections. It promised to resolve a complex of troublesome agricultural problems—stable farm income at a fair level, better diet, cheaper food, fewer surpluses, better conservation, fewer controls. The more the Secretary thought about it, the better he liked it. Maybe this was the key, the magic key, to the development of a sound and prosperous agriculture!

O. V. Wells, it may be noted, was on record as lacking enthusiasm for compensatory payments. Although conceding that "there may be conditions under which the use of commodity payments might well be preferable to direct price support," he doubted, in many cases, "if the payment proposal would automatically lead to the 'clearing' of the market." He also pointed out, "Americans generally simply do not like to feel themselves dependent upon direct subsidies or government checks except as a last resort." There were, he thought, "sound grounds for this opposition, both cultural and operational." [50]

On the basis of this statement, Wells must have had some questions concerning the use of compensatory payments on the broad scale proposed by the Secretary.[51] Possibly he may have felt that price supports for meat, dairy products, and potatoes fell into the category of "conditions under which the use of commodity payments might well be preferable to direct price supports." At any rate, he did not argue against the Secretary's proposal. During the seminars, the pros and cons of compensatory payments had been thoroughly explored. Apparently Wells felt, as a career public servant, that it was not his responsibility to go beyond this and attempt to restrain the Secretary from the decision which his best judgment dictated.[52]

The potentialities of compensatory payments and high-level supports for livestock helped the Secretary make up his mind to reject the two-price system which the National Grange and some others were advocating as a method of dealing with impending grain surpluses. The Grange proposal, employing a certificate plan by which to manage the movement of wheat not needed for the domestic market into the world market, was discussed, but not seriously considered. The International Wheat Agreement was about to be consummated (with the Department's blessing), and it would constitute an export subsidy palliative for the wheat surplus problem.

The two-price system might also result in the lowering of total farm income—particularly that of the grain farmers—and this was precisely what the Secretary wanted to avoid. Most important, however, was his conviction that a vigorous income-support program directed toward the expansion of the livestock industry was clearly superior in meeting the problems of grain surpluses and of sustaining high-level farm income.

A strong price and income support system had one major defect, as Brannan saw it. It would strengthen the biggest commercial farmers, who would be able to produce unlimited amounts, expand their operations, and squeeze out more and more family-type farms. How could something be worked out which would prevent this from happening, and at the same time actively strengthen family farming in America? In his seminar remarks, Brannan had indicated that he was considering a way to scale down government assistance after a certain amount of per-farm production had been protected. Where should the breaking point be, and by what formula would it be determined? The Secretary asked Wells to define a family farm, and Baker to work out a formula giving effect to the definition.

The Census of 1945 provided a bench mark from which to work. Noting that 2 per cent of the farmers produced about 25 per cent of the nation's farm output, and further observing that these 2 per cent produced, per operator, in excess of $25,000 worth of commodities annually, the Secretary settled on this somewhat arbitrary figure as a basis for devising a formula.

Three or four different formulas were worked out, all centering around a unit system. Corn was selected as the commodity yardstick, since it was grown more widely in the United States than any other important commodity. The formula finally agreed upon used 10 bushels of corn as a unit, with the Secretary proposing to support up to 18,000 bushels of corn, valued at approximately $26,000 in terms of the income support standard. For other crops, a unit would be that amount of a commodity which, at the support standard, would equal the value of 10 bushels of corn.

The Secretary and his assistants were well aware of one serious weakness in this scheme. The profit margin on the sale of $26,000 worth of corn would be much higher, say, than on $26,000 worth of eggs, since the cost of production would be much larger on the latter. Working out an ideal system, however, was recognized as a staggering job, since accurate cost-accounting studies have not been applied to this field. Area economic differentials would also make the establishment of a sound national formula an exceedingly complex job, to say nothing of the political difficulties of expounding the Plan to the satisfaction of the nation's farmers.

The problem, then, of working out a really equitable income limitation formula proved too formidable for the Secretary—partially because of the limited time available for producing the forthcoming testimony. But the principle had been formulated and Congress, if it saw fit, could work out further details.

While the emphasis on a livestock economy was looked upon by the Secretary as a major conservation advance, he was not satisfied to stop there. Some of the areas most in need of conservation improvements were those in which livestock was not, and perhaps could not become, an important industry. Furthermore, Brannan's experience with the dust bowl had made a deep impression on him. Land may be private property, but to the Secretary it was also more than that. It was the vital heritage of future generations. No man had a right to abuse his land at the expense of his children and children's children. Far less had he a right to claim government assistance while engaging in farming operations detrimental to the long-run interests of our people.

The Secretary decided, therefore, without any lengthy deliberative process, to require that government assistance programs be reserved for those who complied with such conservation criteria as the Department might establish. In addition, eligible farmers would be required to abide by such acreage allotments and marketing quotas as might be established.

Little consideration was given to the agricultural economists' suggestion that direct payments should be extended to storable as well as perishable commodities. Brannan hoped that high livestock supports would create a demand for grain which would keep grain prices above support levels, thereby obviating the economic hazards of high level supports in this area.

There was general satisfaction among the tobacco and cotton producers with the present program, and no public dissatisfaction with the grain support program remotely approaching that which was associated with price supports for perishables. To suggest direct payments as a substitute for price supports in the field of storables would only complicate his "selling" job, as the Secretary saw it. Better to concentrate on the areas in which the farm program was in trouble than to jeopardize the success of his entire testimony by introducing too many radical changes.

The draft of the testimony was finished only a few days before its delivery before Congress. Upon its completion Brannan took it to President Truman, who went over it with him in some detail. Brannan pointed out that the 1800-unit rule was a "hot potato" which might touch off considerable opposition. The President hesitated on this feature, but when Brannan assured him that the Department was behind the proposal, he agreed to go along with it.

On April 6 Brannan invited the leaders of the major farm organizations to his office and handed them copies of the impending testimony. Meanwhile, other copies had been sent to the chairmen and ranking minority members of the Senate and House agricultural committees. The next day, the Plan was formally launched on what was soon to become a most stormy political sea.

ANTECEDENTS

Allan Kline, president of the American Farm Bureau Federation, reputedly dubbed Brannan's proposals the "Brannan Plan," whereas Brannan himself referred to them as "the Department proposals" or "the administration farm plan." In the light of what has been related, what are we to conclude? Was the Plan a distinctive product of Brannan's mind, or the matured consensus of the best thinking in the Department?

It can be categorically stated that neither the Department of Agriculture nor major elements within the Department were ever on record as favoring inflexible price supports as a permanent peacetime policy prior to April 7, 1949. It is true that at the annual meeting of PMA in St. Louis, Missouri, in December, 1948, a committee on price support endorsed fixed 90 per cent of parity supports for basic commodities. However, the membership of this committee was composed exclusively of state-level officials, and it was in no sense authorized to speak officially for the parent agency. Furthermore, the support level which it endorsed was lower than that proposed by Brannan.

Except for this single instance of deviation within one of its units, the Department had consistently favored flexibility in price supports and moderate levels of support. Senator Anderson's statement that the principles of the Aiken Act were in line with policies which the Department had long desired [53] appears to be correct.

It could be argued that while the Department had not previously favored Brannan's high and inflexible [54] supports, its leading figures had changed their minds by 1949 and were now thinking along lines parallel to those of the Secretary. It is the inescapable conclusion, however, from a study of the way in which the decisions of the Brannan Plan were made, that these decisions represented the thinking of Brannan himself, rather than being the joint product of top officials in the Department of Agriculture. The Secretary, as previously indicated, made his major decisions on the basis of his own best judgment. He did so after hearing a good deal of discussion and debate, but it would be a misconception to conclude that his decisions were built upon the predominant opinions expressed by those participating in the seminar meetings.

It is the impression of those taking part in the seminars that there was general agreement on the desirability of switching from a support formula based on parity prices to one based on income parity. However, there was no discussion of an income support standard such as Brannan later proposed. The use of direct payments *in some cases* seems to have met the approval of most of the members, after a rather intensive discussion. Similarly, there was considerable debate and general affirmation of the principle of tying government benefits to soil-conservation requirements.

On the questions of fixed versus flexible price supports, and on moderate versus high support levels, there was only a limited amount of discussion. No clear-cut consensus emerged on these points, insofar as the participants recall, and certainly there was none on behalf of the principle finally embodied in the Brannan Plan.

Finally, the question of limiting government benefits to a fixed volume of production was not brought up at all, other than for the comment of the Secretary himself during the sixth meeting.

Most of the Secretary's major decisions, then, were not a distillation of Department opinion. Nor did the Secretary make these decisions on a tentative basis and submit them to the critical examination of leading departmental figures before crystallizing them. Even the usefulness of the five-man "cabinet" which helped the Secretary with his testimony was confined to deciding how best to implement the major decisions already made. This was not an insignificant role, but it does underline the fact that the "Brannan Plan" was really Brannan's plan, rather than an organizational product.

The manner in which it was formulated contrasts with the way the long-range testimony offered to Congress in 1947 was drawn up. The latter was the co-operative product of leading technicians and operating officials of all interested bureaus, and the draft of the testimony was submitted to all bureau heads for approval. But in this instance the Secretary made his decisions, drew up his testimony, and turned it over to the President for approval without consulting most bureau heads. His excuse for this procedure was that there was not time to do otherwise, since he had already strained the patience of the Congressional committee chairmen. The farm organizations had refused to testify until the Secretary came forth with his recommendations, so the chairmen were becoming importunate.

Actually, the excuse appears to be rather lame. Brannan apparently knew well in advance of April 7 what the main outlines of his recommendations would be. There was nothing to prevent him from calling leading Department officials together for a general discussion of the broad principles of a program he was inclined to support.

As the chief policy-planner of the Department, it was of course his responsibility to make the final decisions on the basis of his own judgment. But surely it is sound practice for an executive officer to submit policy proposals to appropriate advisers for free and open criticism prior to settling on them. This Brannan did not do, either with the working group immediately surrounding him or with the bureau heads.

If the Brannan Plan appears to be rightly named, where did Brannan get his ideas? It is rare that political proposals originate with the public officials who propose them. In nearly all cases, they are appropriated from others and recast by politicians or administrators to meet a situation which appears to call for them. The Brannan Plan was no exception. As Representative Clifford R. Hope said: "The Brannan Plan does not contain any new or revolutionary ideas. Everything included in it is either in existing legislation or has been the subject of considerable discussion in agricultural circles." [55]

In view of numerous suggestions that the plan to substitute direct payments for price supports in the field of perishables was a dark administration plot to make the farmer more directly conscious of the beneficence of the State, a conspiracy to bind him with chains of gold to the Democratic party, and a shameful attempt to reduce him to degrading dependence upon a paternalistic State, it is noteworthy that the idea had previously been endorsed by some of the most distinguished, conservative, and—in many instances—nonpartisan leaders of our nation.

Agricultural economists, like other academic personnel, are notoriously allergic to partisan politics. Yet they had been recommending direct payments in lieu of price supports for many years. As the Committee on Parity Concepts of the American Farm Economic Association said, in November, 1947: "There is general agreement among agricultural economists that such income supports as are undertaken should be in the form of direct payments to producers rather than manipulation of market prices." [56] The published views of many leading agricultural economists support this statement.[57]

Interest in and approval of compensatory payments was not confined to professional agricultural economists. During the war James Byrnes, then Director of War Mobilization and Reconversion, suggested the use of direct payments instead of price supports in appropriate instances.[58] Fred M. Vinson, who succeeded Byrnes, echoed his sentiments.[59] The Committee for Economic Development, composed of leading businessmen, had also affirmed its postwar support of the principle of compensatory payments.[60] Members of the National Planning Association, whose board comprises twenty-one representatives of business, agriculture, and labor, had likewise taken an affirmative interest in direct payments.[61] Even the task force on agriculture for the Hoover Commission recommended their use.[62] Finally, the Dairy Industry Committee, comprising a large number of prominent dairy industries, had approved their use in the dairy industry.[63]

Moving over to another area, we find that the annual convention of the Congress of Industrial Organizations, assembled in Portland, Oregon, in November, 1948, had adopted the following resolution: "To avoid waste of foodstuffs and to avoid excessive government purchase of price-supported farm products, the Administration should be empowered by Congress to substitute direct parity payments to farmers in lieu of government loans or purchases so that market prices may be allowed to fall below the support level when this is necessary to move exceptionally large supplies into consumption." [64]

Sentiment for direct payments was' by no means unknown to the Department of Agriculture prior to Brannan's day. Howard Tolley, former director of BAE, virtually admitted that he favored their use.[65] It can be safely asserted, in fact, that every departmental study on price policy during the later war years and early postwar years at least considered the possibility of using direct payments as a device for supporting farm income.

Even Congress was not immune to the attractions of compensatory payments. The House Special Committee on Postwar Economic Planning issued a report entitled *Postwar Economic Policy and Planning,* in which it recommended "a system for cushioning declines in prices and income in the event of a business recession, by use of price or *income* supports, or other devices." [66] (Italics mine.)

The Department had also had firsthand operating experience with the general principle of compensatory payments. During the days of the first AAA, direct payments were made to farmers in return for acreage reductions, although the objective was to raise income, not to permit lowered prices. Parity payments of several hundred millions of dollars were made annually from 1938 to 1941 to compensate farmers producing basic commodities whenever price supports failed to bring their income to a "parity income level" corresponding to farm purchasing power from 1909 to 1914. Finally, the income of sugar-beet growers had for many years been supported by direct payments to growers who abided by certain marketing quotas and met other prescribed conditions.

Thus the concept of replacing price supports with direct payments was anything but novel, or the brainchild of scheming politicians with a "statist" bent.

The substitution of an income support standard for the parity-price support formula had a substantial amount of indirect precedent. The word "indirect" should be stressed, since concepts of "income parity" and an income support standard are substantially different. Both use income rather than price as the pivotal consideration, but there the similarity ends. "Income parity" formulas propose to maintain a stable ratio between farm and nonfarm income, while the income support standard represents a relatively fixed income goal, rather than a ratio. That is, Brannan's standard, instead of allowing farm income to *decline proportionately* to a decline in nonfarm income, would *maintain* farm income at a high level as a means of stabilizing the economy as a whole.

Brannan's standard was not completely inflexible, of course, since its moving base and purchasing power factors permit some changes in the income goals. But it was much less sensitive to changes in nonfarm income than is envisioned by income parity proposals. At any rate, in replacing price criteria with income criteria, Brannan was moving in a direction blazed before him by numerous students of agricultural policy [67] and toward a goal enunciated in the agricultural acts of 1936 and 1938.

This goal was redefined in the Hope-Aiken Act, also. Speaking on the floor of the Senate on April 7, 1948, Senator George D. Aiken said: "The proposal to put supports on an income rather than a commodity pricing basis also is set forth in the 1948 act. . . . There was incorporated in the 1948 law a definition of parity. Although this definition had no substantive value at the time, it was intended as a directive to the BAE to seek a method by which parity of farm income might be determined." [68]

The recommendation to tie soil-conservation requirements to price supports had a considerable history of discussion. Writing in the *Farm Policy Forum* of October, 1948, Milton Eisenhower, then president of Kansas State College, proposed that "we should make all governmental economic aid to the individual farmer conditional upon that farmer's establishing and maintaining a conservation program for his farm." [69] The Committee on Parity Concepts of the American Farm Economic Association,[70] Professor John D. Black,[71] and Professors Working and Norton [72] had suggested a similar approach.

Dr. H. H. Bennett, chief of the Soil Conservation Service of USDA, had stated that ". . . application of land technology is certain to spread around the world either voluntarily or by decree." [73] Professor Charles Hardin confirmed the tenor of Dr. Bennett's remarks with his comment that "coercion has been implicit in much thinking about soil conservation." [74]

The suggestion for limiting price support and direct payments to a fixed amount of production had substantial precedent, both in theory and practice. America's traditional bias for the small farmer has been reflected in the homestead laws, which since 1862 have largely restricted homesteaders to 160 acres. This same philosophy, although its application has been under heavy attack, has also found expression in the 160-acre limitation (320 acres for man and wife) on the eligibility for water rights from public irrigation projects in the West.

The AAA operated under rules which scaled down direct payments to the larger farmers. The agricultural conservation payments program also had limitations on eligibility for individual benefits which were once set as low as $500 per farmer, but which later were set at $2,500. Direct payments to sugar-beet growers in 1950 were graduated downwards from 80¢ per 100 pounds for production of less than 350 tons of sugar per farm to 30¢ per 100 pounds for production in excess of 30,000 tons per farm.

Academic antecedents applying more directly to Brannan's 1800 unit rule also exist. John D. Black, discussing the application of a system of direct payments to agriculture, said: "It may also be pointed out that the program as outlined will make large supplementary payments available to our larger farmers, who ordinarily need little or no financial help in their adjustments. This objection could be met, if it were important to do so, as under the AAA—by scaling down the rate of payments percentagewise after a certain level is reached, such, perhaps, as $1,000." [75]

The Committee on Parity Concepts of the American Farm Economic Association took much the same position, arguing that "there are valid objections against large government payments to very large producers such as those operating corporation or nonfamily type farms." The Committee, however, declined to recommend that the latter receive no protection at all, although conceding that considerable sentiment existed for such a position.[76]

Income protection for producers of perishables had been an objective of numerous commodity groups, farm organizations, agricultural economists, and Congressmen since almost the beginning of the program for "basics." The latter were originally given preference because: (1) they were in chronic surplus, from a free-market viewpoint; (2) their producers were the best organized and were represented by the most powerful members of Congress; (3) there were special difficulties associated with supporting perishables because of their nonstorable character. The feeling was widespread, however, that it was unfair to accord a specially privileged position to one group of producers, and that some way should be found to grant equality of protection.

Fixed, high-level price supports as a permanent feature of national agricultural policy, on the other hand, did not have a history prior to 1949 either of serious consideration or of endorsement by leading students of agriculture or by farm organizations. During the extraordinary conditions of wartime, 90 per cent of parity price guarantees met with little serious resistance. Partly, no doubt, this was because market prices were so far above 90 per cent of parity levels that the supports were largely inoperative. Partly, too, acceptance grew out of the certainty that whatever stimulus they provided towards greater production would meet a genuine need rather than provoke troublesome surpluses. Similarly, there was general approval for the two-year postwar extension of the 90 per cent level, since the farmers were believed to deserve this protection while "readjusting" their production patterns to peacetime needs.

But during the brisk flurry of agricultural planning which preceded the passage of the Agricultural Act of 1948, a surprisingly small amount of support was given to inflexible, high-level supports as a permanent national policy. The writer, in fact, was unable to discover a single important organization—farm or nonfarm—or a prominent agricultural economist who, prior to November, 1948, endorsed such supports as sound national policy. Many Congressmen favored fixed 90 per cent supports for basics, and a few agricultural economists concurred;[77] but, on the whole, informed opinion overwhelmingly rejected the concept.

THE NATIONAL FARMERS UNION AND THE PLAN

In view of the repeated charges which have been made that the hand of James G. Patton was writ large upon the Brannan Plan,[78] and that the Plan represented a major triumph for the Farmers Union, it is instructive to review the relevant policy positions taken by this organization during the war and postwar period preceding the emergence of the Brannan Plan. Was the Brannan Plan, in reality, the outgrowth of Farmers Union planning, rather than of planning in the USDA? If it was, did the Plan represent the governmental flowering of long-standing Farmers Union principles, or did it reflect views recently acquired by that organization?

During the early postwar years, Patton was by no means convinced that high-level price supports were necessarily desirable. Testifying before the House Committee on Agriculture in 1947, Patton said: "Every dollar of every price boost gives roughly 90¢ to those farmers who are better off, and 10¢ to those who most need increased income. The result is that the children and the land that are the long-time victims of rural poverty become progressively more disadvantaged."[79] Furthermore, the Farmers Union president asserted: "We want to maintain a free exchange market. If loans, for example, continue to be set at 100 per cent you would pretty nearly eliminate the free market."[80]

Patton's testimony on the Aiken Bill not only confirms this general outlook, but also directly endorses the principle of flexible price supports. During the course of Congressional testimony on April 15, 1948, he declared: "We believe that S. 2318 constitutes a landmark in . . . legislative efforts and we strongly hope that a bill of this general character will be adopted by this Congress. . . . A major contribution of the measure, of course, is its proposal of a new system for the support of agricultural prices in which the level of support is related to the volume of supplies of each major farm product. *The theoretical base of the proposal is admirable.*" [81]

Somewhat later in his testimony, Patton reaffirmed his belief that the Aiken Bill was a "constructive" measure that would "work to the best interest of agriculture." [82]

In 1947 Patton recommended commodity loans on perishables as well as on storable commodities. But Congressman August Andersen (R–Minn.) questioned him as to his views on the prize-winning essay for the American Farm Economic Association in September, 1945, which advocated: ". . . that the price level on farm commodities in this country should be permitted to sink down to the world level and that the producers in this country should receive compensation out of the Treasury for the difference in income that they receive, on a world-level basis, and the amount fixed for what the income should be . . ."

In his testimony Patton answered as follows: "In the first place, I do not think you would get enough money in the Treasury, with the present rate of expenditures, to do that type of thing. . . . Third, I do not think it would be a healthy thing. I believe sincerely that the farmer should receive a fair exchange price for his commodities." [83]

It is thus clear that in 1947 Patton was opposed to permitting a free market for farm commodities, with direct payments to farmers compensating them for the difference between their sale-value and a Congressionally determined "fair value." On the other hand, the Farmers Union was the only major farm organization which did not oppose the use of wartime farm subsidies.[84] Russell Smith, legislative secretary of the Farmers Union, further testified before Congress in 1944 that "a carefully guarded program of subsidies in the postwar period must assure farmers a decent return for their labor, and consumers a minimum adequate diet." [85]

The principle of direct payments to farmers was, then, in line with Farmers Union thinking at a fairly recent period, but it was not linked with a free market.

During the hearings on long-range agricultural policy, Patton made a number of observations of special interest in connection with this study: "Upon the family farms grow independent, strong, alert citizens. The family farm is the final stronghold against oppression, whether economic or political and no tyranny or 'ism' will ever thrive in a country that grounds its agriculture on that base. Such an agriculture is the most efficient, too, from any sensible economic point of view. . . . the family farm—that economic unit upon which our democracy was based in the beginning—is disappearing. Twenty-five years ago less than a fourth of our land was in farms of more than 1,000 acres. Now 40% of all the farm land in the U.S. is embraced in such farms." [86]

At another point in his testimony Patton advanced the opinion that government aid to assist farmers in getting a minimum family income should be conditioned upon adherence to certain conservation goals.[87] He contended that permanent price-support protection should be extended to producers of perishables as well as producers of storables. Loans should be made "as now at the percentages of parity specified in the Steagall Amendment. But the commodities would not necessarily be sold at those prices," Patton suggested. "Rather, they would sell in the price range agreed upon by the bargaining committees of farmers and consumers. The resultant loss would be borne by the Treasury." [88]

During the 1948 campaign, the Farmers Union gave President Truman vigorous support. As an organization with an uncompromising liberal ideology, and one which felt it had been instrumental in obtaining the appointment of a Secretary of Agriculture who spoke its language, it could be expected to follow no other course. If more reasons were needed, it was apparently impressed with President Truman's promises to do his best to keep farm prices up, although it should be said again that at no time did the President pledge his support for a repeal of the Hope-Aiken Act.[89]

Shortly after the election, the National Executive Committee of the Farmers Union met at Denver. The *New York Times* reported: "The committee announced its program after exchanging views with Secretary of Agriculture Charles F. Brannan. . . . The committee called for . . . a stable, not a sliding floor under farm price supports as a guarantee of full parity for farm products." [90]

Reporting on the convention of the Farmers Union Grain Terminal Association at St. Paul, Minnesota, on December 14, 1948, the *National Union Farmer* said: "More than 200,000 northwest grain farmers have served notice on Congress that they want nothing less than 100 per cent of parity on farm price support. . . . Secretary of Agriculture Charles F. Brannan told the delegates he favored a strong price program and said that, 'I shall fight with all my strength any notion that farmers must lead the way to a lower scale of purchasing power.' " [91]

Persons familiar with farm politics and farm personalities noted with interest, at President Truman's inauguration, that the Agricultural Committee for the President's Inaugural Program was heavily sprinkled with leading officers of the Farmers Union. Not a single representative of the National Grange or Farm Bureau was included, but James G. Patton, M. W. Thatcher, Russell Smith, Glenn Talbott, and Homer Duffy—all "big wheels" in the Farmers Union—were among the twelve members of the Committee. A number of the other members were identifiably sympathetic with the Farmers Union.

In February, 1949, the *National Union Farmer* featured a story on Patton's testimony before the House Committee on Agriculture:

Over the last year . . . the Farmers' Union has been engaged in evolving a new approach to the whole matter of supporting prices of agricultural commodities. We have not worked out all of the details of this program as yet, but one thing we are absolutely sure of and that is that the farm program finally enacted by this Congress should provide for the receipt by family farmers of 100% parity. . . . Let me suggest to the committee, for example, that it would be entirely possible for the Department of Agriculture to work out for each commodity in the U.S. a volume of production that would equal that of the average family farm, however it may be defined. It would also be possible for Congress to authorize the CCC to make loans on that volume at 100% of parity. . . . these are the lines along which we have been thinking.[92]

It will be recalled that the Secretary, during the course of his portentous remarks in the sixth seminar meeting, expressed an interest in graduating price supports downward, after a certain minimum value of sales had been protected. This was precisely the stand which the Farmers Union was tentatively recommending in February, 1949.[93]

The March issue of the *National Union Farmer* carried another story to the effect that the Farmers Union was recommending a 5,000-unit limitation on price supports, and had called on the Department of Agriculture to work out the precise value of a unit in terms of both perishable and storable commodities.[94]

In March, 1949, the National Planning Association published a pamphlet, *Must We Have Food Surpluses?*, in which Patton, one of the contributors, stated: "The use of high level price supports, with incentives graduated upward from such a level, deserves far more attention than it has received. The lowering of prices to promote shifts has been proved to be a fallacy." [95]

On April 7, 1949, Secretary Brannan presented his Plan before Congress, repudiating flexible price supports and recommending what amounted to 100 per cent of modernized parity price supports, with a unit limitation plan and with income support for all major commodities, perishable and storable alike. It should have occasioned little surprise, therefore, when *US News and World Report*, in its issue of April 22, 1949 (p. 34), commented: "Mr. Patton, president of the National Farmers' Union, has been overlooked as an influence at the Agricultural Department. He has just scored a rather thorough-going victory in drafting the Administration's new long-range farm program."

After the Secretary's testimony, the Farmers Union promptly issued a statement calling the Plan "the boldest and most forward-looking ever to come out of the Department of Agriculture." It was, said Patton, "a milestone both in the struggle to maintain and preserve the family-type farm, and in the effort to tie together the interests of producers and consumers." [96] Commenting on charges that the Farmers Union had fathered the Brannan Plan, the *National Union Farmer* announced: "Secretary Brannan's plan is his own. The similarity between what he proposed and what the Farmers Union asks only comes about because both are interested in family farming and abundant farm produce for consumers, and we are the only farm organization that is." [97]

Should the Brannan Plan, then, be properly referred to as the Patton Plan? Or is the explanation offered by the Farmers Union correct and adequate? Both men agree that they engaged in general discussions on agricultural matters at various times when the Department was working on the Brannan proposals. Both deny, however, that they worked the Plan out together. [98]

The Brannan Plan, of course, could be the Patton Plan, whether or not the two men carried on policy consultations during the early months of 1949. Patton's views were already well known to Brannan, and the latter had caught up with the latest Farmers Union thinking during his meetings with the Farmers Union Executive Committee and the Farmers Union Grain Terminal Association shortly after the election. Presumably, too, Brannan read the organizational paper.

It could be argued, on the other hand, that the Brannan Plan was the Black Plan or the Plan of the Committee on Parity Concepts of the American Farm Economic Association. Both had endorsed direct payments; both had indicated the propriety and advisability of conditioning benefits upon the carrying out of certain soil conservation practices; both had suggested a scheme for scaling down benefits to the biggest commercial farmers; both were interested in a parity income approach. It must be emphasized, however, that there were fundamental differences between their proposals and those of Brannan. They would have applied direct payments to storable as well as non-storable commodities, which the Brannan Plan did not suggest; they would also have restricted direct payments to depressions.

Insofar as the Brannan Plan reflected concern for the "family farmer," emphasized the correlation of conservation responsibilities to government benefits, concentrated on agricultural abundance and the consumer's interests, extended protection to perishables, and rested on a positive conception of the role of government, it is unwarranted—on the basis of known evidence —to attribute any special influence to Patton beyond whatever contribution his earlier acquaintance with Brannan made upon the latter's thinking. It appears curiously significant, however, that both Patton and Brannan turned their backs on flexible price supports immediately after the 1948 elections, and that they arrived at the simultaneous conclusion that farmers producing both perishable and storable commodities should receive income protection approximating 100 per cent of parity. It is furthermore apparent that the formula for insuring that support benefits went only to that volume of commodities which an efficient family farm could produce came directly from the Farmers Union.

As for the rest of the Brannan Plan, while the Farmers Union could not lay exclusive claim to prior advocacy of its principles, each of those principles was consistent with recent pronouncements made by that organization. Certainly Patton could be pardoned if he believed Brannan had hatched Farmers Union eggs.[99]

THE USDA ROLE IN THE MAKING OF PUBLIC POLICY

The American Farm Bureau Federation was critical of USDA for allegedly concentrating upon policy formulation instead of on administration. The *American Farm Bureau Official Newsletter* of November 14, 1949 (p. 4), for example, stated: "Some of the government agencies . . . muddy the farm policy water occasionally. Roger Fleming, Director of the Farm Bureau Washington offices, suggested that these agencies should stick to their knitting—that of administration."

The Illinois Agricultural Association—one of the Bureau's most powerful bodies—took an even more emphatic position:

"The Association . . . demanded a curb on Brannan's activities in connection with the formulation of agricultural policies. Delegates at the association's thirty-seventh annual meeting approved a resolution condemning Mr. Brannan's effort to promote farm policy originating from the executive branch of the Government instead of from Congress." [100]

Somewhat later, in connection with the USDA-sponsored farm opinion survey (The Family Farm Policy Review), the *Farm Bureau Newsletter* quoted approvingly resolutions adopted by state Farm Bureau organizations containing such sweeping language as follows: "Administrative agencies are not intended to formulate policies." (Maryland Farm Bureau.) "We have long contended that it is no job for federal agencies to tinker with policy." (Massachusetts Farm Bureau.) "Government agencies are charged with administrative functions. . . . Policy making is not their function." (Michigan Farm Bureau.) "Employees of the Department of Agriculture . . . are not employed to help determine basic policies." (Kansas Farm Bureau.) [101]

While the Farm Bureau's national headquarters later insisted that the Farm Bureau was not and is not opposed to active involvement by a Secretary of Agriculture in policy-formulating matters, it clearly sought to leave the impression—during the heat of the struggle over the Brannan Plan—that the making of farm policy was the proper sphere of Congress, farmers and the farm organizations.

Senator Anderson, strangely enough, appeared to share this view. Noting that "it was not the job of government agency personnel to formulate agricultural policy," Anderson went on to say, "We must recognize the very human temptation for government agency personnel to engage in other activities than that of administering farm programs." He concluded: "I want to see farm legislation developed by farmers through their own farm organizations in co-operation with members of Congress." [102] According to this analysis, the Department's policy-formulating responsibilities must be very limited indeed. [103]

This poses a question. Was the formulation of the Brannan

Plan a break with the past, a direct plunge into the policy-making pool by a Department which was formerly concerned with the administering, and not with the making, of law?

It is illuminating to look back upon the part played by the Department of Agriculture during previous major revisions of national agricultural policy. Unfortunately, this is one of the largely uncharted areas of American political history. No one has yet undertaken, to my knowledge, a thorough study of the policy-formulating process, and of the variety and intensity of pressures which went into the creation of the agricultural acts of 1933, 1938, and 1948. Some evidence is available, however, which indicates that the Department of Agriculture played a considerable role in each instance.

The domestic allotment plan, which formed the core of the AAA of 1933, "developed through study and discussion by a small group of economists and aroused considerable interest in the winter of 1932–33 in both farm and non-agricultural circles. M. S. Wilson, recently Undersecretary of Agriculture . . . and John D. Black, professor of economics, Harvard University, developed the domestic allotment plan with the aid of specialists on the staff of the Federal Farm Board and in the Department of Agriculture." [104]

Theodore Saloutos and John D. Hicks, in their *Agricultural Discontent in the Middle West, 1900–1939*, observe that: "Just who was responsible for drafting the AAA bill . . . is not quite clear. George Peek wrote that 'the bill was a composite of ideas contributed by Tugwell, Morgenthau, Ezekiel, M. L. Wilson, some other professors and economists and perhaps Henry Wallace. It was not the farmers' measure.' " [105]

Chester C. Davis, outlining policy development during this period, states that "economists inside and outside the D.A. took a hand in shaping the AAA of 1933." [106] From another source we learn that:

With Roosevelt elected president, the chances for the passage of some kind of domestic allotment bill grew brighter. . . . But much to the disgust of the new administration, the big farm organizations were still divided. Then something happened. "On December 12 and 13, the most representative group of farm leaders ever assembled in the United States met in Washington's Hotel Harrington and there behind locked doors conferred long and earnestly with Henry Morgenthau, Jr. . . . publisher of *The American Agriculturist* and Roosevelt's right-hand man in agricultural matters. When the doors were unlocked a political miracle had come to pass: the various farm organizations had come to an agreement. They would unite in support of Domestic Allotment." [107]

Although the evidence may not be conclusive, it appears that the farm organizations settled upon a program which neither they nor Congress had originated, and which the Department of Agriculture had played a considerable role in formulating.

As for the Agricultural Act of 1938, it is well known that Secretary Henry A. Wallace was an ardent advocate of the "ever-normal granary" prior to its adoption.

According to Philip Aylesworth, formerly Secretary of the Policy and Program Committee of USDA, the Department in more recent years had followed the general practice of passing on its more important policy proposals to the various farm organizations. If the latter were impressed, they would incorporate the Department recommendations into their subsequent testimony before Congress.[108] This was not an iron-clad rule, of course, since the Department regularly testified before Congressional committees on agricultural legislation, and inevitably conveyed some ideas to Congress which had not been screened through the farm organizations.

A major deviation from the general practice, Aylesworth adds, took place when the Department's planning studies in the post-war period crystallized into the testimony on long-range agricultural policy and programs presented to Congress under Secretary Anderson in 1947. Apparently no farm resentment was stirred up by this testimony for several reasons. The major policy recommendations of Secretary Anderson were: (1) a program of abundance instead of scarcity, (2) governmental measures to stimulate consumption, (3) a flexible program of price supports with essentially moderate support levels.

None of these recommendations was of a character to stimulate farm organizational antipathy at the time. Generally speaking, the farm organizations were thinking along similar lines. Besides, Secretary Anderson, while indicating that supports should not be as low as the 52 per cent minimum in the 1938 Act, nor as high as the 90 per cent maximum in effect at that time, took care to testify as follows: "This brings us to the question of mandatory or flexible supports, especially for the basic commodities. We believe that this is a question for the farm people, the farm organizations and the Congress to decide." [109]

While Anderson made some specific recommendations, it could not be accurately stated that his testimony constituted an "agricultural plan" comparable to that of Secretary Brannan's. It was, rather, an estimate of the situation, with certain guideposts thrown in to indicate the general drift of departmental thinking on farm policy.

The Aiken Act, drawn up after the fullest consultations with farm organizations and outside experts, commanded remarkably unified support from the farm organizations and from the administration. The latter's endorsement of the Act was all the more extraordinary in view of its enactment by the Republican 80th Congress, the Congress which was later scored by President Truman at almost every whistle-stop in the nation. As for the role of the Department of Agriculture, Congressman Hope has stated flatly: "The fact is that the Aiken bill was largely written down in the Department of Agriculture. . . . The Aiken bill . . . was the product of the Department of Agriculture and the Committee on Agriculture of the Senate." [110]

In summary, we can safely say that while the Department had spawned many an idea affecting basic agricultural policy, had made important substantive contributions to leading pieces of agricultural legislation, and had presented many of its ideas directly to Congress, no major "plan" had heretofore emerged from the Department, bearing the Department label, and seeking major changes in the agricultural policies of the nation.

THE BRANNAN PLAN: A POLITICAL PLOT?

Did Brannan and his assistants conceive of their handiwork as a project which would become known as "The Brannan Plan," split the farm front, precipitate a major furor in agricultural (and nonagricultural) circles, and cement farmers and laborers in a solid alliance within the Democratic Party? Or did they wish merely to evolve a set of recommendations which, regardless of their fate, would at least stir up some salutary and fruitful discussion by proposing a bold and fresh approach to meet a grave national problem?

The latter is the official Department position, naturally enough. According to Wesley McCune, Brannan and several of his assistants planned to take a short vacation after the presentation of the testimony to Congress, little anticipating the storm which was about to break. There was, he said, no great sense of exhilaration or expectancy on the part of the planning group. A job had been done, and after a brief rest from the intensive work of the past two months, other work would presumably claim their major attention.

This may have been the attitude of some of the men working with Brannan, but it is highly doubtful that it represented Brannan's state of mind or that of all of his major aides.

The Extension Service, commenting on the Plan in a memorandum to extension directors on April 8, referred to the Secretary's statement as a "major USDA policy paper." And Ralph Trigg's letter of transmittal to state PMA committees, several days before Brannan's appearance before Congress, noted that "the entire statement is of great significance, and you will want to study it all with great care." It appears, therefore, that important elements of the Department looked upon the testimony as an event of the first magnitude; and it is unlikely that Brannan and his immediate assistants felt otherwise. There is no evidence, however, that they anticipated the extent or violence of the turmoil which the Brannan Plan stirred up.

Among members of the working group, there had been relatively limited discussion of the larger political implications of the testimony. Virtually no discussion took place, they agreed, concerning the impact of the program on the Democratic party, or upon the possibility of wedding farmers and labor unions into a potent political alliance.

It was of course inevitable that the probabilities of public acceptance should enter into many of the discussions concerning the major decisions which were being made. The planning group, for example, recognized that rice and peanut growers would be unhappy, since their preferred position was eliminated. They were sure tobacco growers would be pleased with the substantial support increases proposed for major tobacco types. They anticipated opposition from livestock organizations, for reasons to be dealt with later. They expected sympathetic attention from the Southern Congressmen who backed the Hope title of the Hope-Aiken Act. Opposition from the largest farmers was taken for granted, although a favorable response from consumer-conscious groups was expected. And, according to McCune, a hostile reaction from the Farm Bureau and National Grange was not anticipated. (This, as we shall see later, represented something short of candor or else surprisingly poor political judgment.)

All of these points were commented upon at one time or another *after* the decisions affecting these groups had already been tentatively made. On the surface, therefore, the tail of political implications did not wag the substantive policy dog. This does not, of course, reveal what may have been in Brannan's mind when he made the major decisions which jelled into the Brannan Plan.

A few comments are in order concerning the secrecy surrounding the formulation of the Plan. Enemies of Brannan suggested that the secrecy which preceded the Plan's unveiling was proof that the Secretary was hatching a dubious political scheme, and that there was something highly improper about the whole proceeding. As a matter of fact, there was no effort to maintain any secrecy whatever during the seminar sessions. Those who wanted to know what was going on were able to do so, and the Secretary indicated no desire to keep any of the discussions in confidence.

The "cabinet" sessions were another story. According to Brannan's associates, he naturally wanted to prevent leaks to the numerous persons who, in Washington, are forever seeking to read the political horoscope. Until he himself had settled upon his testimony, he was anxious to prevent gossipmongers from distorting his thinking, and arousing false hopes and apprehensions. The charges of exaggerated secrecy, it is said, came primarily from those who guessed badly (as most seers had done) what the Secretary was going to say. Whether by accident or design, Brannan appears to have selected a group of assistants who knew how to hold their peace.

Inasmuch as Brannan warmly defended the role of the Department in formulating and presenting his Plan, it is amusing to note that during the long-range hearings on agricultural policy in 1947, Brannan noted with satisfaction that "the Department of Agriculture was working on a long-range policy which would 'not be dressed up overnight in the government buildings in Washington' but would be developed from consultations with farmers at meetings all over the country." [111]

II

THE ECONOMICS OF
THE PLAN

In seeking to persuade Congress and the public of the merits of his Plan, Secretary Brannan built his case primarily upon three general propositions. These were: (1) the favorable effect of high-level farm income upon national prosperity and agricultural abundance, (2) the inhumanity and economic falsity of the "sliding scale" philosophy, (3) the desirability of an income support method encouraging the maximum consumption of our agricultural abundance.

The Secretary pounded away tirelessly on the theme that depressions are "farm-led and farm-fed." Time and again, he declared, the ark of national prosperity has been sucked under the waters of depression by an undertow of sharply declining farm prices and farm income. Farm prices broke first and farthest after World War I. The same thing happened in the early days of the Great Depression. This ominous phenomenon, he maintained, was in the process of repeating itself. "In March of this year farm prices were 15 per cent lower than they were at the beginning of last year," Brannan observed, "while prices paid by farmers were down only 2 per cent from the peak reached last summer. . . . Farm purchasing power turned downward in 1948 and is now at the lowest level since 1942." [1]

As farm prices continued to decline, the Secretary could cite even more disquieting figures. Speaking before the National Farm Institute on February 18, 1950, he said: "Farm prices have dropped an average of almost one-fourth in less than two years. They are still going down. But farmers still have to pay within five per cent as much for what they buy as they paid two years ago. In 1947, farm operators had a net income of nearly 18 billion dollars. Last year, it was down to around 14 billion. The forecast for 1950 is for a net income of under 12 billion dollars. That is a decline of one-third in net farm income at a time when national income is at or near its all-time peak." [2] How far down can farm income be permitted to slide without jeopardizing the national interest? Is this the time to inaugurate the sliding scale, which permits farm prices to drop still further? The Secretary made these points again and again in his chosen role as Paul Revere for American agriculture.

The Secretary frequently invited attention to the fact that "the average net income of farm people from all sources was only $909 per capita, including the value of home-produced food and income from nonfarm sources, compared with the nonfarm average of $1569." As farm prices continued to decline, he was able to point to the still more impressive figure of $763 as against $1,555. The burden of his argument, however, rested not so much upon farm inequality as upon the nation's stake in maintaining farm income at reasonable levels.

All up and down the Main Streets of the Nation, there is hardly a place of business that does not prosper when the farmer prospers. Nor would it be easy to find a person working on Main Street who doesn't get hurt when farm income falls below the point of adequate return.

Last year, for example, farm families spent several billions of dollars on cars and trucks and their operation and upkeep. That spells jobs. That spells profits. They spent additional billions in constructing and repairing farm buildings. More billions went for farm machinery, for feed and supplies, for taxes and rent. All in all, it is estimated that farm cash receipts of more than 27½ billion dollars last year, when translated into farm spending, provided jobs for some nine million workers in industry. . . . That's why I say that the well-being of every proprietor on Main Street, of every factory or white-collar worker, of every professional person, yes, the well-being of *everybody* is intimately tied up with farmer welfare.[3]

To Secretary Brannan, the public had a major stake in establishing a program which would slay the economic dragon of falling farm prices—or at least put a firm bit in its mouth. The way to do the job was to give *effective* income protection to the farmers. This meant not just protection for the producers of storable commodities, comprising only a quarter of total farm output; it meant protection to producers of *all* important commodities. Since this was perhaps impracticable for the present, he would provide immediate coverage for the ten most important commodities, whose annual sale value totaled three-fourths of all farm income. But he wanted it made clear that the protection claims of other commodities should not be disregarded.

The Secretary struck out at the Aiken Act because, while it purported to give protection to meat and dairy products, that protection was extremely precarious. Support for these commodities was discretionary with the Secretary of Agriculture, and restrictions placed upon the use of funds by the CCC put price support operations on a shaky basis.

Brannan did not go so far as to contend that national prosperity balanced on a one-legged stool of farm purchasing power: "Farm price supports cannot substitute for good markets that come with full employment and foreign demand, and, I believe, almost every farmer now understands the importance and relationship to farm prosperity of good wages for city and industrial workers." Nor did he fall back upon the once widely circulated myth that national income is mystically seven times farm income, with the protection and beefing up of farm income sufficient in itself to guarantee good times.[4] But he did believe that maintenance of a high level of farm income would play a major part in stabilizing the national economy.

His attitude could probably be accurately characterized as being midway between the one-to-seven thesis and the view, held by many economists, that an efficient and prosperous productive segment anywhere in the nation helps the entire nation, but that no segment is necessarily more basic than another.[5]

Despite his previous endorsement of flexible price supports, Brannan proceeded to make a direct frontal assault on the entire philosophy underlying them. This philosophy was founded on the assumption that lower price supports for crops in surplus supply would persuade farmers to shift over to crops in shorter supply. The price support structure, in other words, would be locked arm in arm with the "natural" laws of the marketplace except that they would act as an adjustable safety net when prices threatened to fall too far. Thus the free market, although its effect would be somewhat modified, would continue to play a dominant role in balancing production and demand.

The Secretary hacked away at the very roots of this theory. He cited statistics to show that the price system did not operate according to such classical economic dogma.

From 1919 to 1922, potato prices dropped from $1.94 to 66 cents per bushel, but acreage rose from 3.3 million to 3.9 million before it turned down in 1923. Again, from 1929 to 1932, prices fell from $1.32 to 38 cents per bushel; but acreage went from 3.1 million in 1930 up to 3.5 million in 1933. The story is about the same for wheat. From 1920 to 1922 prices fell by almost one-half, but acreage in 1923 was only 5 per cent under 1920. From 1925 through 1928 prices went down while acreage went up. The price fall continued into 1932, but with only minor changes in acreage.

Price is also an unreliable mechanism for adjusting cotton acreage. Following a year of 29 cent cotton, farmers had some 40 million acres in that crop on July 1, 1924; and following 6.5 cent cotton they had some 40 million acres in cultivation on July 1, 1933. Following the Supreme Court decision nullifying the Agricultural Adjustment Act of 1933, cotton acreage went from 28 million acres (in 1935) up to 34 million acres (in 1937), despite the fact that prices fell from 11 or 12 cents in 1934 and 1935 to only about 8.5 cents in 1936.[6]

The real effect of flexible agricultural price supports, Brannan charged, was to give legal sanction to the use of economic hardship as the means of coercing farmers into production adjustments: "If and when the sliding scale *should* happen to work, its effectiveness would depend on starving farm families into adjustment. I think this is cruel—materialistic—un-American. I think it is an implicit denial of the worth and dignity of man."[7]

Another result of applying the sliding scale, the Secretary said, would be: "A great many farm owners and operators would soon be well on their way toward becoming managers or wage hands for individuals and corporations who held the mortgages . . . what some people call a 'flexible' support program, the program which ties a sliding scale of supports to commodity supplies—could slam the door of opportunity so hard that a great many farm families might never get it open again." [8]

The better way, as Brannan saw it, was to keep the minimum price guarantee at a "fair" level and use selective price supports at still higher levels to attract farmers into desirable alternative production patterns. The following exchange is illustrative of his thinking on this point:

Mr. Pace: "Is nòt the fundamental difference in the philosophy of your plan and the philosophy of the Aiken bill that instead of driving a producer out of the production of that commodity by a reduction in support, you lead him out of the production of that commodity into the increased production of the commodity that is needed by raising the support on that commodity?"

Mr. Brannan: "That is right." [9]

This idea derived directly from the wartime experience with forward pricing at high levels for commodities for which heavy increases were needed. As the Secretary put it: "There are ways of directly encouraging shifts in the pattern of production without going through the starving-out process. We learned a lot about this during the war. We developed a system whereby farmers could devote their facilities and their labor to the production of those commodities which were most needed. They set new production records year after year, and best of all, they produced the kinds of goods we needed. Many of us heralded this as a great achievement. . . . We need not reserve all our best efforts for war." [10]

The Secretary had still other objections to the sliding scale. He contended that assurance of fair prices is the best guarantee of abundant production: "Low prices do not encourage efficiency. It takes money to buy new machines, more fertilizer, better seed. It takes more cash to buy electricity than to buy kerosene for the lamps. . . . Our big spurts in efficiency have come in response to high prices, not low prices." [11]

Brannan felt that the natural stimulus of a good income upon technological progress would be supplemented by normal human reactions. Why should farmers work hard, do their best, and turn out bumper crops for our growing population if their only reward was to be falling prices? Speaking ironically before a gathering at Michigan State College, he said: "The way to get more steel production is to raise steel prices. But the way to get farm production is to let the farmers' prices go to thunder."

If good prices promote efficiency and abundance, is not abundance the best assurance of fair prices for the consumer? This point, Brannan said, was often overlooked when the level of farm price supports was being debated. The consumer has just as great a stake in effective price support as has the farmer.

As a parting shot, the Secretary observed that flexible price supports failed to give real financial protection when farmers most needed it. Given short supplies, when farmers do not need price protection, they would probably get 90 per cent of parity under the Aiken Act. Given abundant production, the support level would drop to levels providing negligible protection. To Brannan, this just did not make sense.

Even if Brannan's attack on flexible supports was conceded to be irrefutable, it should be noted that this would not necessarily vindicate his income support standard. Brannan, however, usually defended the price and income support provisions of his plan by generalized attacks on flexible supports and by arguments which were equally adapted to the defense of high-level supports based on the formula embodied in Title I of the Agricultural Act of 1948.

Brannan's twin goals of guaranteed farm income at a relatively high minimum level and increased consumption of meat, eggs, and dairy products were potentially incompatible. Prices which would bring an expansion of meat and dairy products would prevent low income groups from consuming the volume they needed and wanted to buy. This is where production payments would come to the rescue. If prices for these priority commodities were permitted to sink to their natural level in a free market, with the farmer compensated by direct payments for the difference between the market level and a "fair" level, the farmer could receive his just deserts without burdening the consumer.

As for the taxes which this would entail, far better that farm income be sustained directly from public funds than indirectly through a system of price supports which (1) applied a "consumer tax" in the form of artificially high prices, (2) required undisguised taxes to maintain the very price support system which raises grocery bills, (3) forced the government to buy huge quantities of food and place them—at least temporarily—beyond the consumer's reach.

His objective, according to the Secretary, was just the opposite of Henry Wallace's. Instead of killing little pigs, he wanted the people to eat them! Furthermore, government purchase and storage of perishables carried the ever-present hazard of spoilage. Public indignation over such a development, combined with public resentment over artificially maintained high prices, might seriously jeopardize the entire program of supports for farm prices.

This, then, was the principal rationale for the Brannan Plan. In practically all of his discussions of the Plan, Brannan drew upon these stock arguments, although he occasionally garnished them with one or more of the following contentions. The 1800-unit rule was defended as a reasonable policy, consistent with the historic American tradition of supporting the family farm. Brannan presented it as a logical evolutionary outgrowth of precedents in our public land policy, in the management of public irrigation projects, and in limitations upon other types of agricultural payments. Capitalizing upon public dissatisfaction with some of the large potato checks, the Secretary argued: "I can find no justification for, or public policy served by, the payment of more than $400,000 in price support money to one potato farmer."

Since no public official—in 1949—seemed able to propose a

public policy without identifying it with the battle against communism, Brannan frequently cited the family farm as a bulwark against communism.

For those who said the 1800-unit rule would penalize the efficient farmers, Brannan had a ready answer: "I am for efficiency of production, and for constantly increasing our efficiency. But I do not agree with those who hold that the only path to efficient production is industrialized mass farming. I want to see no collectives taking over the farms of America—whether those collectives be of the Soviet design or the corporation pattern. I believe the family-sized farm can be efficient, and I believe that we should concentrate our efforts for increased efficiency upon the family-sized farm unit because of the important human values it contributes to our society. I am for encouraging, strengthening, and preserving the family-sized farm as the backbone of American agriculture, not turning our backs upon it and destroying it in the false name of increased efficiency." [12]

Invoking the mighty symbol of private enterprise, he deplored the fact that the government was becoming "a bigger and bigger operator in the food business. We want to encourage free enterprise by taking the Government out of the channels of trade just as far as possible—out of warehousing, processing, shipping, and marketing, permitting dealers and consumers alike to have the benefits of free markets on the perishable products of our farms, as long as we can still make all farmers more secure in their right to a decent and fair reward for their toil." [13]

From another angle, he deprecated the Department's obligation to purchase perishables and feed them back into the market at appropriate times: "I just do not want to try to be—or I think any Government people should not be—sitting in a position of trying to determine when to put things back into the market in order not to force the commodity down below the support level, and thereby force us by another process into the market. I just think there are so many dangers in there for us that it puts us in the position of the ordinary speculator in the market. We are not too anxious to get into that kind of position." [14] (It should be noted, however, that the Secretary's objections logically apply to storables also. The CCC faces precisely the same problem in administering the price-support program for "basic" commodities.)

On several occasions the Secretary alleged that his Plan would promote the interests of foreign trade. When questioned on this point by Senator Anderson, Brannan said: "I would respectfully submit that my Plan would be advantageous to world trade." This was so, he believed, because perishables would operate in a free market and because the price support standard would encourage the steady production of sufficient quantities of agricultural commodities to insure that foreign countries would have regular access to supplies beyond our domestic needs.

The contribution of the Brannan Plan to the interests of conservation was another of the lesser arguments used by the Secretary in defense of his proposals. This contribution, as we have seen, was based on the soil conservation requirement and on the emphasis on livestock agriculture, which would automatically encourage the diversion of tilled land to legumes and pasture.

Finally, Brannan made occasional reference to the advantages in his Plan from a nutritional point of view. Greater consumption of meat and dairy products was consistent with long-standing recommendations of dietary experts.

A CRITIQUE OF BRANNAN'S CASE

The Secretary's claim that his Plan would serve to dike the flood waters of depression fares poorly under close analysis. Direct payments made to farmers producing perishable commodities under the Brannan Plan would presumably come from general tax receipts. To the extent that these payments represented contributions by farmers themselves, there would be little or no economic effect. Insofar as payments came from taxes paid by nonfarmers, they would represent a reduction in the purchasing power of this group precisely proportional to the increase in the purchasing power of farmers. The net result would be to leave the total national purchasing power unchanged—

unless it is assumed that payments would be made from borrowed money. Brannan did not make this assumption, at least not publicly.

Similar doubts arise concerning the application of the income support standard to storables. Farm income for producers of storables would indeed be kept high by the Brannan Plan, but to the extent that prices remained above normal market levels, consumer purchasing power would be correspondingly reduced. The consumer who pays 10 per cent more for his corn or his wheat has his purchasing power reduced as directly as the taxpayer who pays an equivalent 10 per cent in the form of taxes to directly supplement farm income.

Professor T. W. Schultz has labeled Brannan's plan for preventing depression as "not appropriate." [15] He joined other economists in the view that the Plan was not counter-cyclical, since the support standard was set so high that even with relatively full employment, income payments would be made to segments of the farm population. Such payments make no contribution to preventing depression. The volume of payments would be so much larger in depression, however, than during prosperous periods that they would have a partial counter-cyclical effect—*if* the payments were deficit-financed.

Any notion of a unique correlation between farm purchasing power and national prosperity has been pretty well shattered by national economic developments between 1949 and 1956. Although farm income dropped sharply during those years, the size of both the working force and of the national income steadily increased. Farm income shrinkage may be partly attributable to the declining percentage of farmers in the nation, but this does not alter the apparently indubitable conclusion that the nation can prosper even if farm income declines sharply.

Because of the tendency of farm prices to drop much faster during recessions than the prices of industrial goods and services, most economists agree farmers deserve special economic attention. It is one thing, however, to equalize the farmers' comparative position with other economic groups and quite another to put them in a highly preferred position. A major depression would inundate many other groups while leaving farmers, under Brannan's income support standard, high and dry on a plateau of relative prosperity. There seem to be no justifiable grounds, economic or otherwise, for singling out farmers for this kind of treatment.

Brannan's income support standard could be criticized on other grounds than its relative freezing of abnormally inflated farm prices into the farm program. As was pointed out by Roy R. Green in a temperate and illuminating analysis of the Brannan Plan for the National Association of Manufacturers, "The fact that conditions of war and inflation caused the prices of and the income from (certain commodities) to rise abnormally above the price of and income from other farm products that were in less urgent demand, is no justification . . . for attempting to hold such price relationships indefinitely." [16] Furthermore, Brannan's income support standard would tend to maintain these commodity relationships "regardless of whether new production and marketing techniques would dictate that the current price should, in fact, be lower than in the base period." [17]

The Brannan Plan did permit the Secretary of Agriculture some discretion in adjusting price supports in order to maintain desired price relationships, but if this power were used, another problem would arise. To quote Mr. Green further, "If it were deemed necessary and advisable . . . to lower the price support standards for an important group of the nonstorables such as livestock, it would appear necessary to raise correspondingly the price support standards of another important group of commodities in order to end (a given year) with farm income totalling [the desired figure]." [18]

Proceeding to Brannan's thesis that flexible price supports do not bring about appropriate production adjustments, some contradictory evidence is found. Dr. Black stated flatly: "If Secretary Brannan was right the other day in discussing flexible price support effects on production adjustments, I would have to say that all the teachings on this point in all the universities in the U.S. are wrong." [19] Black produced examples demonstrating that price differentials do influence farmers' production plans. He showed that when cotton prices dropped in 1930 and 1931, Southern farmers shifted substantially from cotton to corn, and that when corn prices dropped, they went back to cotton. Furthermore, he said: "Out in the real wheat and flax country, where it is largely either one or the other and mostly wheat, there is a very important relationship of flax and wheat prices that affect wheat acreage. . . . The conclusion that one has to come to after such analysis is that flexible prices will produce shifts in the acreage, and in the output of different individual crops." [20]

Professor Schultz came to the same conclusion: "Under conditions of full employment both theory and practice provide no support for the view that relative prices will not bring production in line with demand." [21] He conceded, however, that there are some areas where the land is adapted to only one or, at most, several commercial crops. Equipment needed for producing these crops may be both expensive and ill-adapted for use in other types of agricultural production. In these areas, falling prices will not necessarily bring about any important change in the production pattern.[22]

Albert T. Goss, former Master of the National Grange, although a firm defender of flexible price supports, agreed that they would not in themselves bring proper readjustments in wheat. "We believe that the same government which fostered the expansion of wheat so vigorously will probably be able to find ways for aiding readjustment which will not leave a trail of bankruptcies in their wake." [23] Elsewhere Goss said: "We do not believe flexible floors can be applied alike to all commodities. There must be flexibility in their use."

In studying Brannan's attacks on the "sliding scale," one notes an apparent failure to discriminate between periods in which all or most farm prices are falling and other periods in which price declines affect some commodities far more than others. Obviously, a distinction must be made. Where prices for major farm crops fall in a fairly uniform manner, it is hardly to be expected that farmers will reduce acreage of the particular cash crop they normally grow. Where price declines are selective, presenting the farmer with relatively attractive alternatives to his present production pattern, he will of course try to take advantage of better income possibilities.

The Secretary did make one concession, of a sort, to the flexible principle. In the bill drafted by the Department to embody the Brannan Plan, authority was included to permit the Secretary to alter the price support standard for meat, eggs, and dairy products by as much as 15 per cent in order to maintain desirable feed ratios.

Implicit in Brannan's over-all philosophy of production adjustments is at least a limited recognition of the adjustment value of *downward* flexibility in support levels. Brannan, as we have seen, proposed to establish price supports above his minimum level when necessary to bring about production increases of certain commodities. It may be assumed that these ultra-high supports would be allowed to decline after supplies had been sufficiently—or excessively—augmented. Presumably Brannan felt that price declines which did not fall below his minimum income support standard would help bring appropriate adjustments, but that this influence would mysteriously vanish when prices fell below his standard.

Experience in recent years, it should be added, indicates flexible price supports have serious limitations because of factors not stressed by Brannan.

When farm production is excessive in the aggregate, which seems to have become our normal peacetime condition, flexible price supports may work to reduce some surpluses only at the expense of creating others. That is, if price support reductions on surplus commodities reduce the acreage planted to those commodities, the land taken out of this type of production is promptly replanted to other crops. Thus, surpluses are only transferred from some commodities to others—in the absence of an effective land retirement program.

The second prong of Brannan's attack on the "sliding scale" grew out of his insistence that high-level price and income supports were essential to insure sufficient production to meet the nation's needs. The consumer is best served, he urged, by a guarantee which will assure farmers that full production will net them a fair per-unit return.

Professor Schultz has demonstrated that agricultural production remains remarkably stable under almost all conditions.[24] The depression years of 1929–33 reduced the production index for agricultural commodities by only three points. The droughts of 1934 and 1936 cut over-all agricultural production by only about 10 per cent. Neither the prewar nor the postwar acreage reduction programs brought about a reduction in total farm output (or even, in most cases, a reduction of output in the commodities under restriction).

Despite farm price declines of 16 per cent from 1952–57, total farm output has risen 6 per cent during this period. Even with the soil bank in operation, and with severe acreage slashes in many basic commodities, and with marketing quotas in effect for all basic commodities for which Congress has authorized such quotas, farm production in 1957 equaled the all-time record and was 8 per cent higher than in 1951–52 and 13 per cent higher than in 1947–49. High prices or low, rigid supports or flexible, acreage allotments or no acreage allotments, Benson or Brannan, American agriculture continues to set new production records under the imperious urge of technological progress.

It is logical that total farm production should not respond very much to price levels—except as these affect the farmers' capacity to take full advantage of advancing technology.

No individual farmer, as one of about 5 million producers, can hope that an acreage reduction on his part will have a measurable effect on the market price. It can only reduce his personal return. Since overhead costs remain relatively fixed and since the market price for crops is always uncertain, farmers automatically tend—at all times—to make the maximum use of their resources. It is to their self-interest to do so. Farmers produce in the anticipation that they will net *something,* and the greater their output the better their chances for getting a larger something.

The fact remains, however, that the assurance of reasonably

good prices, combined with the degree of farm prosperity growing out of those prices, does promote a more rapid introduction
of improved agricultural technology, and hence promotes agricultural productivity.[25]

Farmers who are assured of reasonably good prices in the fall
are more willing to go into debt to buy more or better farm
machinery as well as more fertilizer, insecticides, etc. This effect,
combined with the tendency of guaranteed high-level prices to
bring more marginal land into production, or keep it in, means
that high-level supports do have a positive effect on total farm
production.

Brannan was right, therefore, in saying that his support standard would promote greater agricultural abundance. But with
overproduction a chronic and vexing national problem, the
benefit is dubious. On the other hand, supporters of flexible
price guarantees who concede the above line of argument must
concede that flexible supports tend to cut farm output, at least
partially, only at the price of reduced agricultural efficiency.

Brannan's accusation that a "sliding scale" is harsh and inhuman is more the language of the crusader than of the objective student of agriculture. The entire free enterprise system
depends (in theory, at least) on the directive effects of the free
market upon production. If the sliding scale, which actually
moderates the natural effects of the free market, is "harsh," then
the pricing system on which our entire economy rests is doubly
so. Admittedly, agricultural prices are more responsive to supply
and demand than are industrial prices. They are so responsive,
in fact, that they sometimes actually interfere with orderly
adjustments of agricultural production.

Admittedly, too, agricultural prices may drop so much faster
than the prices of things the farmer buys that farm income falls
to intolerable levels. A strong case can be made, therefore, for
the assumption that the rigors of the free market fall with unwarranted severity upon agriculture. But this is not the same as
saying that any price movements below Brannan's support
standard or 90 per cent of parity are harsh and inhuman.

The Secretary's fulminations against flexible supports were

largely based on his belief that they were callous devices for forcing people out of agriculture by making the lot of the marginal farmer unendurable. Anything which causes or permits lower farm prices can have this effect, to a limited extent. But most agricultural economists agree that the grave problems of the chronically low-income farm families can not be solved by a price support policy of any conceivable kind. Their distress primarily grows out of productive incapacity, not out of price. Farmers who haven't much to sell do not find their living standards materially affected by price supports, whether those supports are high or low. Furthermore, flexible price supports in no way preclude the employment of a variety of other methods (some now being tested by USDA) for improving the productivity of these farmers or helping them obtain suitable jobs off the farm.

What are the merits of Brannan's contention that his Plan would promote maximum consumption of America's present and potential agricultural abundance? When defending his proposals for production payments as an alternative to purchase and storage, Brannan conveniently compared their use with alternatives under Title I of the Agricultural Act of 1948 (calling for high-level supports); but when discussing coverage and income support, he contrasted them with Title II (calling for flexible supports).

There is not much doubt that, at equally high levels of income protection through price supports or production payments, consumption would be greater if prices were allowed to settle to their natural levels. On at least some products, and certainly for those on which Brannan proposed production payments, sufficient elasticity of demand is present to insure that lower prices would enlarge consumption. Still, this is not tantamount to saying that the Brannan Plan would increase consumption more than the Aiken Act.

The Aiken Act, as Brannan himself noted, provided only indirect and relatively uncertain price support for meat, eggs, and dairy products. Supports for these might vary between 60 and 90 per cent of parity, requiring a relatively limited fiscal commitment. But the Brannan Plan, by requiring income support for these commodities at about 100 per cent of parity, could have effects on consumption quite unlike those anticipated by Brannan.

Production payments, as contrasted with a price support scheme, transfer a substantial portion of the costs of a farm program from consumer to taxpayer. Under a price support program, taxpayers pay the considerable costs of buying up farm commodities and carrying storage costs. As consumers, they also pay higher prices for food because of the price-jacking effects of this program. Thus the farmers' improved income position grows out of subsidies from both taxpayer and consumer.

Production payments, on the other hand, would put the entire burden of farm subsidies on the taxpayers' shoulders. Even though consumer subsidies constitute a form of regressive taxation (a fact not understood by most people) and even though they deplete the pocketbook quite as much as direct taxation, they are less conspicuous and hence less disagreeable to most Americans. Given a choice between maintaining a hidden tax on the consumer or substituting a direct tax in its place, most politicians would instinctively choose the former.

Thus, Dr. Black was probably correct in commenting that: "Secretary Brannan can say that his production payments will keep down prices to consumers and encourage consumption, but I shall have to say: Not without larger expenditures on production payments than Congress will ever provide. Hence we are sure to get wide production control out of the Brannan Plan." [26]

This was a very serious charge, and one that Brannan never really tried to answer. Certainly *if* Brannan's income support standard were maintained, there would be a strong probability that production controls would be initiated to reduce program costs. If so, this would hardly lead to the abundance, and hence the consumer gains, Brannan hoped for.

Brannan himself anticipated the possibility of extended controls by including them in the bill drawn up by the Department, and admitted that "marketing quotas or similar feasible devices may be desirable for meat animals, dairy products, poultry and eggs." [27] In a number of instances, he emphasized that he was not proposing to subsidize unlimited production.[28]

Since Brannan was anxious to encourage meat, milk, and egg production, it is strange he gave so little attention to the advantages of applying the production payment principle to corn and wheat growers. Permitting the price of these commodities to fall to lower market levels would benefit farm consumers of wheat and corn, encourage more livestock production, and thus tend to reduce grain surpluses. Growing costs of middlemen might still have brought disappointing results to consumers, but lower grain prices (along with a lower level of perishable price guarantees), would have given the Plan its best opportunity to demonstrate its potential consumer benefits—and also its best chance to keep over-all costs at bearable levels.

Some authorities question whether lower market prices for perishables would actually bring appreciable advantages to the consumer. A state extension service director, for example, observed in 1950 that: "If the farmer gave away his wheat, a 16¢ loaf of bread would cost 14.7¢. If he gave away his wool, $50 suits would still cost $44.30. If a farmer gave away a cowhide, a $10 pair of shoes would still cost $8.63. If he gave away his tobacco, a 20¢ pack of cigarettes would still cost 17⅗¢. And if he gave away his milk, a quart of milk would cost 12¢." [29]

With the percentage of the consumer's dollar spent on farm products steadily decreasing (from over 50¢ in 1947 to about 40¢ in 1957) and with grocery prices refusing to recognize the long slide in farm prices from 1947 to 1956, it is clear that lower market prices for unprocessed farm commodities would not necessarily have benefited the consumer as much as some of Brannan's supporters anticipated. This is not to say, however, that consumer gains would have been insignificant if the Brannan Plan had operated under a lower income support standard. On some commodities, and at some times, those gains would probably have been substantial.

Brannan's opponents raised a host of objections to his Plan in addition to contesting Brannan's major claims.[30] On the whole, the Secretary appears to have badly misjudged the nature of his opposition. He had expected criticism to center on his 1800-unit rule and on the proposal to move from a parity basis to an income support basis in calculating price supports. In explaining his Plan to leaders of the major farm organizations on the day preceding his Congressional testimony, Brannan concentrated on these points. Since direct payments were already authorized under existing law, and had been included in the language of the Aiken Act without protest by farm leaders, he apparently did not anticipate a major attack upon them.

The most publicized charges against the Plan were that it would (1) cost too much, (2) involve regimentation and socialism, (3) expose farmers to the dangers and degradation of federal subsidies.

One of the first questions raised at the Congressional hearings on Brannan's testimony was the cost of the Plan. Most of the questions concerning cost grew out of the proposal to use production payments. Direct payments to farmers had been made before, but never under commitments as firm and as extensive as those pledged by the Brannan Plan. To a lesser extent, the high-level supports for storables also figured in the question of comparative costs between the Brannan Plan and alternative proposals.

The cost issue plagued the Secretary all the way, and sinister implications were attributed to his refusal to make an over-all cost estimate. Brannan did make an initial effort to calculate probable costs on perishables. He detailed Frank Woolley and O. V. Wells to work out the hypothetical cost of production payments for the perishable commodities receiving priority consideration. Woolley declares that when the Secretary looked at the figures submitted to him, he said: "Too high. Try again." A second effort was made, with all doubts favorably resolved in the direction the Secretary wanted. Again Brannan rejected the figures as excessive.[31] Ultimately he submitted estimates on hogs, eggs, milk and milk products, and potatoes; but at no time did he offer over-all estimates on program costs.

The curiosity concerning possible costs was perfectly legitimate, and did not involve merely the badgering which Brannan sometimes seemed to think it represented. There can be no doubt, however, that many of his opponents based their estimates on assumptions of a severe depression, plus an extreme interpretation of every aspect of the Plan having cost connotations. The Department of Agricultural Economics of the University of Illinois was widely quoted as estimating that "the cost of the Brannan Plan could easily be as much as the total federal budget before the war." [32] Representative Hope put the probable cost at more than seven billion dollars annually; Senator Aiken thought it might cost five to six billion dollars; and Senator Taft assumed a cost of about six billion dollars. A research study for the National Association of Manufacturers suggested an annual cost of three and a half to four billions.

Perhaps the most thorough and objective study of the probable costs of the Plan was made by Professor George Mehrens of the University of California. Professor Mehrens estimated the cost at about three billion dollars, assuming the continued existence of those production controls in effect in 1950. In the absence of all production controls, he thought costs might rise to eight billion dollars or even higher.[33]

(Brannan's critics had a tendency to attack his Plan on grounds that it would lead to an appalling increase in production controls. But when denouncing the Plan's cost implications, they tended to assume the existence of no controls at all!)

The Secretary did not deny that his program would be more costly than support operations under the Aiken Act. In his testimony before the House Committee on Agriculture on April 25, 1949, he said: "I am making a comparative analysis with respect to method only. Obviously a lower support price would mean a relatively lower commitment by the Government and thereby lower losses where any losses to the Government occur. It would certainly mean lower income protection to farm people." [34] In defense of his program, however, he stated: "The least expensive program in the public interest, for the long run, will be that which encourages the greatest and most efficient consumption of farm commodities which would otherwise be surplus. . . . The real core of the question of cost is how effective we choose to make our program. . . . Any program which is so designed that the public investment is always sure to be small is going to be an ineffective program at the very time a strong program is needed." [35] He conceded that if there were a major depression, his program would entail heavy expenditures, but said: "Some people may be planning on depression, but the Government of the United States must plan otherwise. By action of the Congress, we are committed to a policy of promoting maximum employment, production and purchasing power. In my opinion, a strong farm program is an essential of that policy." [36] "In the end, we will save no tax money at all by allowing prices to go down to depression levels. Depressions cost more than any conceivable price support can cost in good times." [37] Why, asked Brannan, did no one ask for an estimate of the costs of previous farm programs before they were enacted? "Title II of the Agricultural Act of 1948 provides for the same kind of payments, and no estimates of the cost of that legislation were ever requested or made prior to its adoption. Title I of the Act of 1948 continued the wartime level of price supports, yet no cost estimates were called for or considered at the time of its adoption." [38]

Brannan was convinced that it was impossible to make any realistic estimates of cost. Future production and price levels could not be known, for one thing. If costs appeared to become excessive, production controls would be put into operation. "It should be clearly understood that the only so-called Government controls involved in my recommendations are those which limit the amount of the Government's commitment to farmers."

Marketing quotas, the only effective method of controlling the output of many farm products, could be put into effect only by a vote of two-thirds of the producers, and no one could predict farmers' action in this respect. At any rate, he said, the program could not cost more money than Congress was willing to appropriate.

In the field of perishables, however, the Secretary was certain that the total cost to the public would be less with produc-

tion payments *than under a system of price supports providing
equivalent income protection.* The cost to the taxpayer might
be somewhat higher, but the gain to the consumer would more
than offset it. An important factor, as Brannan saw it, was that
increased numbers of livestock would consume all or part of
our grain surpluses, thereby reducing CCC costs in connection
with storage and general maintenance of its program.

Summing up, Brannan felt that a strong price support program, in fending off depression, would justify whatever it cost.
Besides, he felt that preoccupation with mere tax costs overlooked important social costs in denying people nutritious foods
they needed.

On the difficulties of prognosticating probable costs of program operations, the Secretary got general support from informed persons. Senator Aiken, after making one estimate,
admitted that cost predictions were largely guesswork.[39] Representative Harold D. Cooley (D–N.C.), chairman of the House
Committee on Agriculture, said: "I can agree with you that it
would be almost an impossible thing to determine with any
degree of accuracy the cost of any of these programs. I do not
believe that we have in the past even attempted to estimate the
costs. We have determined what we thought was reasonable and
proceeded with the program." [40] Agricultural economists also
agreed that dollar estimates would be based on so many unknown factors as to be of limited value.

Precise estimates are one thing, however, and comparative
estimates another. The Brannan Plan did propose to extend
effective income protection to producers of 75 per cent of the
nation's farm commodities, as contrasted with producers of
25 per cent of farm commodities under then existing legislation. This in itself would logically enlarge the costs of the program. Since the price support levels were raised well above those
in either Title I or Title II of the Agricultural Act of 1948,
additional costs would doubtless be entailed.[41] Brannan, as we
have seen, conceded as much. Dr. Black put it this way: "One
hundred per cent of parity is going to cost several times as much

as 90 per cent and still more times as much as if the flexible provisions are kept." [42]

Considering the precipitous drop in farm income from about 17½ billion dollars in 1948 to about 11½ billion in 1957 (much of it while high level supports were still in effect), a farm program designed to keep farm income at Brannan's proposed levels would doubtless have entailed prohibitive costs.

Brannan's claim that some perishable products could be handled more economically via production payments than by price supports (assuming an equal degree of income protection in either case) was borne out by several competent studies. Geoffrey Shepherd, one of the nation's leading agricultural economists, made a careful statistical analysis of comparative costs under price supports and production payments for the 1948 potato crop. He concluded that consumer gains would outweigh increased tax costs under production payments by approximately forty-eight million dollars.[43]

The National Planning Association pamphlet, *A Framework for Long-Range Agricultural Policy*, agreed with this position: "It is probable that the economy as a whole would have suffered less waste if the Government's recent commitment to support the price of potatoes had been carried out by production payments instead of by direct purchases accompanied by destruction or diversion to lower valued uses. . . . The money outlay by the Government might have been larger with production payments so that more money income would have been transferred from people as taxpayers to producers of potatoes. But this would have been offset by the reduction in the amount transferred from people as consumers to producers." [44]

In a statement presented to the Subcommittee on Agricultural Policy of the Joint Economic Committee in December, 1957, Professor George K. Brinegar of the Department of Agricultural Economics and Farm Management, University of Connecticut, made the following significant observation:

1. The total cost to the public, paid in the form of taxes and changed consumer prices, of implementing the usual types of agri-

cultural programs would be less under direct payments than under price supports, assuming that a given amount of income is to be transferred to agriculture.

2. However, United States Treasury disbursements would be about three times as great under direct payments as under price supports, again supposing that a given amount of income is to be transferred to agriculture.[45]

This, undoubtedly, was the political nub of the matter so far as Congress is concerned.

One argument on behalf of production payments which was *not* raised by Secretary Brannan was expressed by a number of agricultural economists. This was that production payments would bring the true costs of the agricultural program out into the open, instead of concealing them under a system of price supports whereby consumers unwittingly subsidize the farmer. By eliminating these hidden subsidies, and bringing total public costs into the light, many economists felt that the agricultural program would undergo a more searching legislative scrutiny to determine the extent of the public's interest. A more rigorous pruning of public expenditures for agriculture, of course, was hardly the objective Brannan had in mind!

A final point relative to the social value of production payments deserves attention. Professor Shepherd's analysis of production payments for potatoes includes this significant observation: "There is, however, some difference in who would foot the bill. Our income taxes are progressive. You pay a larger slice of your income as taxes as your income goes up. We have seen that more of the cost of a direct payment program comes out of tax money than with a price support program. Thus, the upper income group of people would pay a larger share of the cost under a direct payment program than if we had a price support program." [46] This is one of the major reasons why some spokesmen for low-income groups favor the production payment system. James G. Patton's bitter attack upon *A Framework for Long-Range Agricultural Policy* was largely directed against its failure to reckon with this characteristic of the Brannan Plan.[47]

Some of the most virulent and politically effective attacks on the Brannan Plan charged that it would "regiment" and "socialize" American agriculture. Brannan's proposal to impose acreage allotments and marketing quotas on supported perishable commodities, when necessary, touched off this aspect of the debate. Apprehensions growing out of this proposal were intensified by the belief that heavy costs would rapidly bring about an imposition of those controls.

The Republican National Committee aroused further fears by widely circulating a speech by Representative Hope in which the latter declared that the Brannan Plan exposed farmers to fines ranging up to one thousand dollars, or imprisonment up to one year, for failure to keep proper reports and records. Said Representative Hope: "My prediction is that if this bill ever becomes a law we'll either have to have more farm bookkeepers or bigger jails." [48]

Brannan's opening Congressional testimony indicates that he was caught off guard by attacks from these quarters. The inclusion of controls for perishables was originally conceived as a routine precaution against extraordinary developments. Brannan had no intention of enlarging and intensifying agricultural production controls. He hoped, on the contrary, to reduce them by reducing the surpluses which give rise to production controls. (His income support standard, however, might have led to grievous disappointment on this score.)

Recovering from his surprise, Brannan replied, "My recommendations call for absolutely no form of authority or control not contemplated by Title II of the Agricultural Act of 1948." The only controls which could furnish any basis for misapprehension, he said, were marketing quotas, and these could be rejected by one-third of the producers involved. So long as controls provided by law were imposed or rejected by the farmers themselves, Brannan thought the farmers were not being "regimented." When you come down to it, said the Secretary, "the legislation I have recommended is less restrictive than any so far enacted by virtue of the fact that it offers more encouragement to the abundant consumption and production of farm products and thereby offers more protection against surpluses.

This program would increase inducements for desirable adjustments without ordering them." [49]

Continuing his counterattack with a thrust at his favorite target—flexible supports—Brannan charged that "holding over farmers' heads the threat of a price cut is the worst kind of regimentation. And it offers them nothing in return for being starved into submission."

Brannan was piqued by Representative Hope's charges that S. 1971, the bill drafted by the Department, contained ominous provisions exposing farmers to harsh legal penalties. In an open letter to Hope, he retorted that S. 1971 actually proposed to *reduce* the penalty provisions of existing laws:

The absence in the present law of a specified penalty for the making of a false report by a farmer did not free him from prosecution for such a violation. On the contrary, this situation made it necessary to prosecute a farmer-violator under the General Criminal Code for committing a felony, which carries the very severe penalty of a fine of as much as $10,000 or imprisonment for as long as five years or both. *By removing the application of the General Criminal Code, S. 1971 makes* the penalty much less severe than under existing law.[50]

Representative Hope, on August 14, 1950, replied in part as follows:

The Secretary inadvertently has let the cat out of the bag. First, he concedes, whether he intends to do so or not, that drastic fines and jail sentences would have to be in the law to make his plan operate.

Second, he discloses that he has not studied the matters of fines and jail sentences, or he would know that S. 1971, the so-called Brannan Plan bill, states in the penalty section that "The remedies and penalties provided in this title shall be in addition to and not in substitution for any of the remedies or penalties under existing law." [51]

Hope clearly misconstrued the law in advancing the line of argument contained in his second point. In the absence of the milder penalty provisions inserted in S. 1971, the Department of Justice would have had no choice in prosecuting persons making false reports but to apply the rather harsh provisions of the

General Criminal Code. However, with specific penalties written into the bill to cover specific offenses, the Department of Justice, in accordance with settled practice, would disregard the Code and carry out the express will of Congress contained in the bill.

The charge that the Brannan Plan would "socialize" agriculture may be summarily dismissed. While many right-wing writers and politicians have assiduously sought to make government regulation and socialism synonymous terms, they have not yet succeeded in altering the dictionary. Persons with political motives or cloudy conceptions will continue to misuse the word "socialism," but their distortions need not detain us here.

On the other hand, the accusation that the Brannan Plan would result in increased government regulation of agriculture has already been conceded to have cogency. With the possibility of production or marketing controls embracing producers of perishables for the first time, and with the high level of support for farm incomes making it probable that these controls would be applied, American agriculture might indeed have been enmeshed in a spreading network of production controls under the Brannan Plan.

In this connection, one of the more serious charges against the Brannan Plan was that it frankly proposed to set up a system of managed agricultural prices. The Plan set high levels of price supports for storables, and provided even higher income protection for producers of meat, eggs, and dairy products. Furthermore, the Secretary proposed to establish selectively higher supports whenever the national interest required increased production of certain commodities.

The latter was consistent with Brannan's basic thesis that while price declines do not satisfactorily adjust production, selective price increases do. It was also consistent with his philosophy of "leading" farmers out of surplus crops instead of "forcing" them out through the operations of free market prices. This approach, however, has significant implications for the economic system under which America has chosen to function.

Most economists do not contend that each instance of governmental interference with the system of free market prices necessarily weakens the free enterprise system. In some instances it may preserve and strengthen it. But they do believe that the operation of relatively free market prices is one of the essential ingredients of a free economic system.

Any system of price supports upsets the equilibria maintained by a free market and introduces an element of governmentally directed production. But there is a vast difference between price supports deliberately set at levels which bring them into infrequent operation or minimize their market effects, and income and price supports at a fixed high-level minimum combined with selective price or income incentives beyond that level wherever production adjustments are desired.

Brannan's philosophy would not have given us a completely administered agriculture, since natural market forces would direct production to the extent that individual prices freely rose *above* his support standard; but whenever individual prices declined below that standard, their directive effects would be cancelled. In periods of falling farm prices an almost completely price-regulated agriculture would follow, and perhaps a production-regulated agriculture also via acreage controls and marketing quotas.[52]

Many persons testified before Congressional committees that middlemen would absorb as profit the bulk of the difference between the lowered market price which the farmer would receive for perishables and the former support price. Heavy pressure would then be brought to bear upon Congress, it was said, to authorize controls over the marketing trade. Some thought it "might require the setting of margins and retail price ceilings, more or less like the war period."[53]

If popular expectations were excessive, and if retail prices dropped only slightly, there would be a temptation for USDA and proponents of the Brannan Plan to explore the possibilities of bringing about greater consumer gains through regulation of the trade practices of middlemen. This temptation already exists, however, since the declining percentage of the consumer's dollar going to farmers, combined with farmer resentment of this fact, makes the middleman a popular target for farm politicians.

No feature of the Brannan Plan aroused as much passionate denunciation as the proposal to support farm income (in part) by production payments. The attack was mounted from many quarters. Production payments were branded as subsidies which would sap the moral fiber of the American farmer. It was felt that government "handouts" would destroy the farmers' independence and self-reliance, promote raids upon the federal treasury, and encourage vote-hungry politicians to promise ever larger federal bounties. Farmers, traditionally our most rugged individualists, would be transformed into bondsmen of the federal treasury, and one of the great sources of America's moral and spiritual strength would be swept away.

The Secretary was partially prepared for this attack. Instead of referring to direct payments as compensatory payments, which the agricultural economists had been doing, or as subsidies—a word evoking unfavorable reactions—he shrewdly labeled them "production payments." Payments were to be made to farmers for *continuing* production at a high rate as an alternative to curtailing production in an effort to balance supply and demand at artificial support levels.

There is really no basic difference to the farmer, said the Secretary, between production payments and the loan and purchase agreements employed by the present farm program. In both cases the farmer receives a government check. The only difference is that the producer of storables can redeem his stored commodity if market prices rise above the loan or purchase level. This rarely occurs. The farmer, therefore, is already receiving subsidies, and no one is making a great fuss about it.

Brannan argued as follows: "Let us be realistic: All aid to agriculture in any form is a subsidy. There is no point in blinking this fact. Rather, let us stand on principle. To the extent that the agricultural subsidy serves the public welfare, it is not only justified but necessary. By the same token, no subsidy is justified which does not serve the public welfare. And if we stand on that principle, we can be open and aboveboard about it; there is no reason for agricultural aid to be concealed or hidden." [54]

The alternatives to production payments, as the Secretary saw it, were either an ineffectual price support system for perishables, or no income protection at all. A price support program would be of little value because support levels would be so low as to provide negligible benefits; or, if high enough, the government would be compelled to buy and store food in such quantities that eventually the whole system would crack up.

Thoughtful critics agreed that the difference has been exaggerated between the present loan and purchase agreement system and direct payments. Under the former system, however, the farmer was able to maintain the illusion that he was getting a market return for his product. This illusion, some of them thought, was important and socially valuable. [55]

The supposed aversion of farmers to direct payments, because of the feeling of dependence which it would allegedly create, was sharply challenged by an opinion poll conducted by the Agricultural Economics Department of Michigan State College. [56] According to its findings, most farmers hold no readily recognizable emotional objections to direct payments. Furthermore, the poll analysts noted: "Farmers who realized that direct payments would eliminate government purchases from processors and handlers were much in favor of using direct payments. . . . Those who recognized that direct payments would reduce waste or spoilage in government stocks also were strongly in favor of using direct payments." [57]

Loren Soth of the *Des Moines Register and Tribune* told the Subcommittee on Agricultural Policy of the Joint Economic Committee in December, 1957, "A number of studies . . . have shown that, contrary to statements by some farm organizations, farmers are not opposed to the direct payment method as a means of stabilizing prices of perishable commodities." [58]

It is quite credible that such distaste for direct federal subsidies as exists among farmers may be outweighed by their aversion to some of the defects of price support, or outweighed by the alternatives of little or no governmental income protection.

This is not tantamount, however, to saying that farmers are indifferent to whether their subsidies are open or disguised. Doubtless they prefer the latter, whenever these are feasible. Certainly other economic groups do, and there is no reason to believe farmer psychology is different.

In this connection, it is important to note that some agricultural economists believe meat and dairy farmers' income can be satisfactorily protected by payments to meat and dairy processors when free market prices fall below a desired level. These payments could be incorporated in the farmers' checks from the processors, thereby protecting farm income and farmers' pride without depriving the consumer of the advantages of lower prices. This administrative device, used in some European countries, helps preserve the farmers' sense of independence (and enormously simplifies the bookkeeping problems as well).

The Farm Bureau blasted direct payments partly on the ground that they would throw the agricultural program "into politics" and make farm income dependent upon annual appropriations. This would unstabilize agriculture and expose it to a position not endured by other economic groups. Dr. Walter Wilcox, who for many years has had first hand experience observing the ways of Congress, voiced similar sentiments when he wrote: "Farmers will have little confidence in a program that requires large government appropriations each year. And with good reason. Because of this political consideration, I place near the bottom of my list of implementing programs the Production Payment Plan we have heard so much about the last few months." [59]

Brannan was scornful of the notion that his Plan would put the agricultural program into politics. The program, he said, is, always has been, and never can escape being in politics. Certainly a lot of politics is involved in determining which products are going to be supported, how they will be supported, and what the level of support will be. It is simply absurd to say that there is no "politics" involved in the making of farm policy.

As for the claim that agriculture would be perilously dependent upon annual appropriations, he pointed out that agriculture is already dependent upon the capital funds of the CCC. Whenever its funds are inadequate for maintaining prices at Congressionally established levels, more money must be voted to replenish its capital stock.

The Secretary was somewhat disingenuous in taking the latter position. Congress is, of course, far more willing to vote increases in CCC capital stock than it would be to vote direct cash payments to farmers. In the former case, there is always the possibility that government advances will be repaid. Thus far, World War II and the Korean conflict have helped vindicate that hope. But there would be no way to recoup Treasury payments to farmers under the production payment system.

The Farm Bureau's opposition to direct payments was based in part on contradictory premises. In the first place, it was contended that farmers would be inclined to vote for Congressmen trumpeting the largest promises. In the next breath, the Farm Bureau alleged that the farmer would be "at the mercy" of annual appropriations—the implication being that the farmer would not fare so well under the latter system. If, as the Farm Bureau then claimed, it was interested in reducing farm subsidies because of their debilitating effects on farmers, the best way to accomplish this would be by bringing all farmer benefits directly into the open, both for perishables and for storables. Economizers could certainly proceed more effectively against goldfish-bowl production payments than against price supports providing an equivalent income protection. That farm leaders understand this was indicated long ago by testimony before a Senate Committee by Ed O'Neal, former president of the Farm Bureau: "Under the Farm Bureau Plan, the Government aid to farm income would be largely indirect and thereby more comparable to that afforded other groups. The Government aid would be reflected in higher prices in the market place for farm products. This would be more acceptable to farmers, consumers, and taxpayers." [60]

This understandable reluctance to shift agricultural subsidies from consumer to taxpayers was one of the principal obstacles faced by supporters of direct payments. Where the alternatives are either no federal aid or inadequate federal aid in a situation of distress, or the accumulation of an unmanageable federal stockpile, direct payments may well prove attractive to Congress. Where agricultural spokesmen can choose between direct payments and an effective consumer-borne program, they will choose the latter on sight.

Production payments had not yet run the gauntlet. In addition to its other alleged vices, it was assailed as a "consumer subsidy." Even the BAE, in a paper prepared for the seminar which O. V. Wells conducted, stated, "If the guaranteed farm return is a fixed point of public policy, it is really the consumer who is being subsidized by the compensatory payment." Why, critics asked, should the government pay part of the people's grocery bill? Why not also pay part of people's rent, clothing, and other expenses?

This argument is based on a misconception. In no proper sense can production payments, as contemplated by the Brannan Plan, be called a consumer subsidy, as BAE should have been the first to recognize. It is a farm *income* subsidy instead.

In analyzing the consumer impact of agricultural price or income supports, it is necessary to work from a base point. That point, logically, is free market prices and the income farmers would receive from such prices. When taxes are paid to maintain a price support system which keeps prices above free market levels, an income subsidy for the farmer is provided largely by means of a consumer penalty. Elimination of the consumer burden through allowing prices to fall to natural levels certainly does not constitute a consumer subsidy. It simply restores the market system to "normalcy." And, if production payments are introduced to raise farm income, they accomplish that end without injuring the consumer. This noninjury is what has been mislabeled a "consumer subsidy."

The point can be further clarified in dealing with the charge, made by Senator Taft and others, that production payments were comparable to the food subsidy system employed by the British during the war.[61] Again, the reasoning is faulty. Using the free market level as a norm, the British payments did represent a genuine consumer subsidy, since prices were artificially held *below* market levels by the subsidy. The subsidy was used to give the farmers what was regarded as a fair income, an income which could not have been obtained with a free market unless food prices were permitted to rise above the levels the government felt low-income consumers were able to pay.

There is, then, a fundamental difference between government payments to maintain farm income while keeping prices *below* market levels, for the benefit of the consumer, and government payments which increase farm income *beyond* what market prices are bringing, for the benefit of the farmer. Removing a consumer burden, as proposed by Brannan, is in no sense the equivalent of the British system of wartime food subsidies.

The Farm Bureau raised the point that if agriculture's benefits were to come via direct federal payments, why should not labor receive similar treatment? Why should not collective bargaining (the supposed equivalent of price supports) be abandoned, the working man get whatever he could from his employer, and the government make up the difference between his wage and a fair wage by direct payments to the worker? Should not the same sauce be served both goose and gander?

Price supports have one likeness to collective bargaining contracts. In both cases, prices (for farm commodities and for labor) are held above the levels which would prevail in the absence of either. However, because there are some resemblances, specific evils growing out of the one and absent in the other should not be disregarded. Collective bargaining does not bring about a wastage of consumer goods, nor does it deprive the people of access to such goods. The production payment proposal was made in the face of impending accumulations of foodstuffs which could not, barring the unexpected (which materialized in the Korean conflict!), be disposed of in the public interest.

Furthermore, agriculture's position in the economy is unique in so many respects it can properly be given special treatment without providing a precedent for giving similar benefits to other segments of the population.

Livestock representatives testifying before Congressional committees on the proposal for a "trial run" for production payments emphasized the tremendous administrative difficulties involved in applying such a system to livestock.[62] That complications would arise goes without saying, but ways were found to manage the wartime subsidy payments, which were similar from an administrative standpoint. Agricultural economists do not generally regard the administrative problem associated with direct payments as insoluble.

A number of Brannan's critics assailed his Plan as injurious to our foreign trade objectives. They contended that his income support standard would put a floor under prices of storable commodities (which account for most of our agricultural exports) at excessively high levels. The consequent widening of the margin between the domestic price level and the world price level would make it difficult for us to maintain that volume of trade essential to the interests of farmers and friendly nations alike.

High support levels encourage the growth of import quotas, since importations competing with commodities enjoying high-level protection tend to drive prices down and hence make support operations more costly. Similarly, if exports are to be maintained, export subsidies must be of sizable dimensions to cover the difference between the domestic and the world price. The higher the support level, the more expensive this operation becomes. As expense increases, the volume of exports itself is threatened.

Brannan took the offensive on this point in his opening testimony. Speaking of the criteria "by which to judge and by which to guide our program," he said: "It must serve general policy objectives, including . . . co-operation with other nations in the interests of peace and prosperity. It can do this by . . . encouraging free-flowing world trade by reasonably assuring sufficient products for export." That is, Brannan fell back upon his major thesis that only high-level price supports will encourage the full production which will enable us to meet our own needs and have adequate and stable reserves with which to supply our foreign customers.

Experience since 1949 suggests that the nation has little cause to fear that lower price supports would imperil the production of the quantity of foodstuffs needed to supply our national and international requirements. Particularly in wheat and cotton, the problem which has proved almost insoluble has been how to prevent an oversupply which depresses domestic prices and leads to demands for "dumping" abroad—in one form or other. The latter can adversely affect the economy of nations which produce the same commodities and thus seriously jeopardize American relations with these countries.

D. Gale Johnson's *Trade and Agriculture* makes the following comparison between the Agricultural Act of 1948, the Brannan proposals, and the Agricultural Act of 1949:

The most important aspect of any of these programs is the level of price supports. On this score, the Agricultural Act of 1948 is by all odds the least likely to disturb international trade seriously. Both of the other proposals envisaged relatively high levels of price supports. The levels would be so high that most farm products would be at or below the price-support level much of the time. Consequently, it is likely that various restrictive devices would be imposed, such as production control, marketing quotas, and marketing agreements. Each device might well require some restriction upon imports or an export subsidy if market prices are to be increased. . . . The higher the level and the greater the degree of interference with market prices, the more pronounced will be the schism between trade and agriculture.[63]

The State Department, in any case, was *not* consulted when the Brannan Plan was formulated.[64]

A further argument against high-level supports, such as those contemplated by the Brannan Plan, stressed the fact that, when applied to selected commodities, they lead to the development of substitute products which usurp the market, sometimes permanently. Or they may encourage a stepping-up of production by foreign competitors, with long-run effects of serious consequence for the protected producer. The Committee on Postwar Agricultural Policy of the Association of Land-Grant Colleges and Universities reported: "The full effect of an increase in the price of a product may not be felt immediately, but sooner or later a part of the domestic market is likely to be lost to substitutes and a part of any foreign market to competing products and sources of supply. Once established, either large-scale production of substitutes or another source of supply may develop and maintain a position of advantage for a considerable period, if not indefinitely. Markets are lost more easily than they can be recaptured. Indeed, when once gone they may be lost forever." [65]

Insofar as the free market–direct payment aspect of the Brannan Plan is concerned, a different picture is presented. As a high State Department official wrote Mr. Brannan shortly after his opening testimony, direct payments as an alternative to price supports would be very helpful in permitting trade to flow more freely, and would reduce the necessity for some tariff barriers. Brannan's later proposal to replace cotton price supports with direct payments might have proved one of the most fruitful aspects of his Plan, through promoting international trade in American cotton and eliminating the need for export subsidies.

The potentialities of this approach were appreciated from the outset by some cotton producers. Wesley McCune has noted that "the first commodity group to enter Brannan's door after his recommendations were publicized was a delegation of cotton men, who suggested that use of his proposal on cotton would . . . let it compete with the world market and . . . let it compete with synthetics." [66] Over the years, the advantages of freer prices for cotton have tended to gain increasing recognition. If the free market–direct payments alternative is ever extended in a major way, cotton may well be an early beneficiary.

One of the major political objections to the income support standard principle was raised by Representative Hope when he said: "I am wondering if, since the public generally has accepted parity prices as being fair prices, if we go to some other basis for measuring the return to the farmer, that we may not be losing

. . . some of the benefits that have accrued because of the acceptance of the idea that parity prices were fair prices, both to the consumer and to the producer." [67]

From a political point of view, this was an impressive argument. It had taken a long time to build the symbol value of "parity" to the sacrosanct status it enjoyed in 1949. (In 1959, it might be added, growing dissatisfaction with the farm program has greatly reduced parity's symbolic utility.)

The legislative stability of the farm price support program rested heavily on the popular belief that parity—no matter how many changes are made in its computation—is somehow mystically fair to farmer and consumer alike. Farm spokesmen were therefore reluctant to abandon a symbol of proven utility for an alternative which superficially offered more, but which might founder on its own generosity and imperil gains won by the farm bloc over a period of decades.

It has been noted that much of the case for Brannan's high support standard rested on his conviction that farmers were not getting a fair share of the national income. The defense of high support levels in general derived (and derives today) much sustenance from the statistic, often repeated by farmers and farm organizations as well as by Brannan, that farmers get a per capita income of only 50 per cent to 60 per cent as much as nonfarmers.

Until the searchlight is turned on the farmers' relative income status and on income distribution within agriculture in 1949, the Brannan Plan can not be soundly evaluated. If farmers were an underprivileged class, and their living standards were well below those of urban working classes, a case could be made for a vigorous governmental effort to redress the inequality.

The question of income distribution is a touchy one among agricultural interests. Professor Hardin has noted that Congress once blocked BAE in its attempt to investigate farm income.[68] Elsewhere he observes that some officials in the agricultural colleges regard the subject as "too hot to handle." [69]

Perhaps the best insight into the subject during Brannan's tour as Secretary was provided by the 1950 Census of Agriculture, as modified by "The Farm Income Situation" for August–

September, 1952, published by BAE. The Census showed that there were 5,382,162 farms in America in 1950. However, 1,032,366 of these were residential farms, which either sold no produce or sold less than $250 worth annually. Another 642,118 farms were operated on a part-time basis, with the operator annually working one hundred or more days off the farm. This left 3,703,128 "commercial" farms.

The average net income from these farms was not given, but reasonably accurate estimates can be made. Since part-time farms include those with a value of products sold ranging from $250 to $1,199, we can strike an average between those figures and assume a cash agricultural return to part-time farmers of around $475,000,000. Assuming another $125,000,000 of sales from residential farms, we arrive at a total cash farm return from noncommercial farms of about $600,000,000.

These figures must be modified somewhat in the light of statistics compiled by BAE. The latter demonstrated that the total value of sales from all farms in 1949 was 27 per cent more than that reported by the Bureau of the Census. This would bring returns from noncommercial farms up to $760,000,000. In addition, non-money income equaled $650 per farm in 1949, giving these farms a possible gross of about $1,860,000,000. Net farm income then approximated 40 per cent of gross farm income, leading to the estimate that noncommercial farms netted in the neighborhood of $744,000,000 in 1949.[70]

Total net farm income in 1949 was $13,593,000,000. Subtracting $744,000,000 leaves $12,849,000,000. Dividing this by 3,703,128 commercial farms indicates an annual net income for full-time farmers in 1949 of approximately $3,470. In contrast, the average annual income for industrial workers in 1949 was $2,862![71]

Several other factors made the comparative income picture even more favorable for farmers. Almost half of all farms are in the South, where incomes and costs for all economic groups average well below the national mean. Professor Black also notes that "the living which the farm family obtains from the farm, including its rent, is rated in such comparisons one-half what these cost in the city, and these make up about one-third of real farm family income on many farms." [72]

It can be argued that the above unfairly reproduces the farmer's comparative economic status because the average full-time farmer has such a heavy capital investment. This fact, it is said, should be reckoned with in calculating the financial returns which a status of economic equality would bring to farmers. The subject of capital investment should, of course, enter into any comparative income analysis, but there are far more cogent arguments for legislation enabling families to maintain minimum standards of health and decency than for legislation guaranteeing a fair return on a capital investment. The two objectives are fundamentally different, and it may be questioned if the latter is ordinarily a proper responsibility of our government. [73] Yet supporters of high-level price or income guarantees are often driven to regard it as such in order to rationalize their position.

The same general considerations apply to unpaid family labor. The farmer's wife and children frequently contribute a substantial amount of labor, for which there is no urban counterpart, to enable the farmer to realize his income level. For public policy purposes, however, this too is a somewhat extraneous factor. The crucial point is that the farm family (using the deception of averages) managed in 1949 to net an impressively larger sum than the average urban working-class family—with one breadwinner.

The phrase "with one breadwinner" alters the picture considerably, of course. Few farm women hold an outside job, while about one-fourth of urban married women were doing so in 1949. Rough calculations indicate that inclusion of this factor sharply decreases, but does not entirely wipe out, the over-all economic advantage enjoyed in 1949 by the farm family over the urban working-class family.

Even in late 1955, after farm prices had undergone a long decline, John D. Black observed that "in dollars of comparable

purchasing power, the incomes per family of family-size commercial farms in the United States are now equal to those of
comparable working family units in the nonfarm economy." [74]

Brannan was technically correct in stating that people on the
farms in 1949 got little more than half as much as nonfarmers,
but this figure provides a superb example of the perils of statistics. In the first place, Brannan included residential farms,
which are really not farms at all. Secondly, he used a *per capita*
figure reflecting the fecundity of rural people. While the latter
can not be ignored in the establishment of any agricultural income goal, its introduction into Brannan's income comparison
seriously weakens the validity of the conclusion Brannan drew
from it. Children cost money, but it does not follow that large
families need a per capita income as large as that of smaller
households. Finally, Brannan included 2,430,000 hired farm
workers in making his comparison. Their incomes are notoriously low.

It remains true that the average full-time farmer netted substantially less than the average *urban family* (as contrasted with
the average working-class family). The average urban family,
according to the *Monthly Labor Review* of August, 1952,
earned $4,300 in 1950 after payment of personal taxes. This
would put it considerably above the average full-time farming
family on the income scale. [75]

In determining the farmer's claim on federal subsidies, however, it seems appropriate to compare farm income with that of
the income of working-class nonfarm families. On the basis of
such comparison, Brannan's favorite statistic provided a badly
distorted picture of the farmer's relative economic status. Certainly support for Brannan's income support standard would
have met with an even more unfavorable reception had it been
made clear that full-time farmers had largely moved out of the
"have-not" class to an economic position several notches above
that of the average industrial worker.

The absolute and comparative income of full-time farmers,
in any event, is less revealing than a further breakdown provides. Dr. Black, quoted by Arthur Moore in the National Plan-

ning Association's pamphlet, *Underemployment in American Agriculture,* makes an exceptionally important observation:

> By lumping the low-income farmers in with commercial farmers for the purpose of shaping policy, the picture is distorted out of all semblance of reality. Simple arithmetic will show what happens. Add the incomes of a group of "medical service workers"; $20,000 for a doctor; $8,000 for a laboratory technician; $4,000 for a nurse; $2,000 for a janitor. The average income for these "medical service workers" is $8,500. Now—by using this average the facts are distorted in two ways: a) The doctor's salary appears to be much lower than it really is, and b) The low income at the bottom of the group is glossed over. Thus, when national averages involving all farmers are used, the commercial farmers are made out to have much lower incomes than they actually have, and the real poverty of the low-income group is tragically covered up. Yet this system of averages has been the common practice.[76]

Returning to our appraisal of farm income distribution, we discover that among the commercial farms [77] 707,723 sold from $250 to $1,199 worth of farm products annually. Another 895,889 sold from $1,200 to $2,499. This means that at least one and one-half million farm families were still in serious economic straits; many of them were desperately poor.

Turning to the balance of the farmers and applying the same statistical method used in determining average farm income, we discover that the roughly 2,000,000 farmers who sold annual produce valued at $2,500 or more netted an average of approximately $6,875 in 1949! [78]

The significance of these figures becomes apparent when we observe that farm price supports benefit farmers in proportion to the value of products sold. That is, those who need help least get the most; those who need help most get the least. And the higher the level of supports, the greater the advantage—both absolute and comparative—accruing to the most prosperous farmers! Professor Hardin came to the heart of the high-level price support program when he wrote that it was heavily warped in the interests of the big commercial farmers. "About nine

million persons on two million farms were the primary bene-
ficiaries of agricultural policy," he wrote in 1950.[79]

His words were echoed by other informed agricultural students. For example, D. Gale Johnson declared: "The present
price programs, when they do result in income gains in agriculture, give the bulk of the gains to farmers in the best economic
position. . . . if cash farm income is increased by 1 billion dollars, less than 25 per cent of the farmers would receive 75 per
cent of the total, whereas about 45 per cent of the farmers would
receive less than 7 per cent of the increased income." [80]

Walter W. Wilcox also observed (in 1956) that "Price stabilization measures are of little benefit to the 1.6 million full-time
farm families with sales of less than $2500." [81]

Brannan proposed to deal with this problem by means of his
controversial 1800-unit limit, partly excluding from program
benefits the 2 per cent of the largest farmers producing 25 per
cent of the nation's commercial output.[82] Limitations on their
price and income protection would have left about 15 per cent
of the nation's output of the ten priority commodities to seek
whatever rewards it could find in the market place. The idea was
applauded by the Farmers Union, and by liberals throughout
the nation who disliked heavy federal subsidies to big farmers
and feared the alleged growth of factory-type farms at the expense of the family-type farms.[83]

Brannan's supporters were overoptimistic on this point, unfortunately. Combined with Brannan's income support standard, an effective 1800-unit rule would have merely stripped
part of the benefits of high support from the top 5 per cent of
the more prosperous commercial farmers, while providing a
bonanza for the other 95 per cent. That is, it would have affected
only about 100,000 farmers, leaving the other 1,900,000 farmers
who netted an average of $5,500 in 1949 to receive the lion's
share of the program benefits.

As it turned out, the 1800-unit rule would not have been very
effective, partly because the Secretary had not thought things
through in putting forth this particular proposal. Asked if his
limitation would apply when acreage controls and marketing

quotas were in effect, the Secretary was caught offguard. After a period of uncertainty, he conceded that when farmers had voted a mandatory program of their own ". . . it seems to me that what they have gone through is a process of determining what production is consistent with the national and foreign demand, and so forth." [84] He would not, he said, apply the 1800-unit rule under these circumstances.

Representative Hope caught the point immediately. "Unless you apply the limitations to those commodities which will be under acreage allotments or marketing quotas, it seems to me the idea might as well be abandoned altogether." [85] Inasmuch as the high level of price supports for storables would almost insure the imposition of acreage allotments and marketing quotas, Hope's point seems well taken.

Representative Pace asked Brannan if it were correct that "the only time you propose to use the payment plan is in those cases where there is a surplus?" Brannan responded: "That is right." [86] Since production controls would probably follow on the heels of production payments to keep costs at a minimum, the 1800-unit rule, as Brannan conceived it, would tend to become inoperative whenever either acreage allotments or production payments were being used. Inoperative most of the time, in other words!

A further weakness of the 1800-unit rule is illustrated by Brannan's admission that his price support standard would indirectly help the big producers of storable commodities even if his limitations were operative. He conceded that "the effect of the loan and purchase agreement is to hold the umbrella over everybody." That is, by holding prices at high levels for storable products, there would be an automatic market tendency to prop the price of the remaining production which had no legal claim upon price support benefits.

Any important limitation of the amount of production to be protected by price support operations runs into another problem, also. The more production that is dumped on the open market, the greater the gap which develops between market prices and the support price level. This in turn encourages more

farmers to turn over their produce to the CCC, thereby intensifying the government's surplus storage problem.

A subsidy limitation plan associated with direct payments and
a free market would not encounter these obstacles, of course,
although the administrative problems involved might still be
imposing.

When Representative Cooley showed a desire to detach the
1800-unit rule from the rest of the Brannan proposals, the Secretary put up no fight whatever. [87] This was in sharp contrast to
his persistent and vigorous battle for production payments and
for a fixed, high-level minimum income support standard.

The 1800-unit rule came under fire from the Farm Bureau
and other groups [88] because it allegedly "put a ceiling on opportunity." This, its critics felt, would obstruct the growth of efficient agricultural production. In turn, this would jeopardize the
very abundance the Secretary desired.

Actually, the 1800-unit rule (if effective) would have done no
more than put a ceiling on the opportunity of the biggest operators to drink deep draughts from the public trough. It is one
thing to allow unrestricted growth of enterprises financed by
private capital and functioning in a free market; it is quite another to allow producers an unlimited opportunity to fatten at
the public expense. Certainly it is dubious public policy to subsidize heavily the most prosperous of our agricultural producers.
Furthermore, it is possible to sympathize with those who view
efficiency as something less than the Baal to which a democratic
society must always bow.

Professor Schultz observed that "the Brannan Plan also has
made it crystal clear that no one—at least no major political
group—is seriously concerned about the problem of the one to
two million farm families who are really poor." [89] Elsewhere,
Schultz advanced this sobering thought: "The Brannan Plan
would probably increase rather than diminish the income inequality that exists within agriculture. Like all price support
approaches it does not come to grips with the widespread and
socially significant problem of poverty imbedded within agri-

culture. Instead, like other pricing measures in this field, it proposes to give economic benefits principally to those farmers in agriculture who are normally fairly well up the American income ladder." [90]

D. Gale Johnson agreed with this analysis, and went on to say: "Not only does a high-level support price program fail to meet the needs of low-income families, but the cost of the program is likely to be so great that it will preclude Congress' taking any action to meet the problems presented by low incomes in agriculture." [91]

Brannan was aware that his program would not satisfy the needs of the poverty-stricken element within agriculture. In his initial Congressional testimony he stated: "The price and income supports I have suggested, in common with all other price-support systems, fall short of meeting the needs of those operators who lack enough good land and enough capital to produce the necessary volume with the necessary efficiency for a good standard of living." [92]

But in defense of his income support standard, he later said that if the submarginal producer does not get "a reasonable return for the commodities he produces, there is no use talking to him about . . . a loan program to expand his productive resources." [93]

Brannan's point is well taken so far as it concerns low-income farmers alone. But it should not be allowed to obscure the fact that the impoverished farmer's need furnishes no excuse for a price or income policy which heavily subsidizes those not in need.

It is interesting to note that James Patton, a fighting liberal, resigned from the National Planning Association [94] when it issued a study criticizing the transfer of income from nonfarm to farm groups under the Brannan Plan. The significant thing to Mr. Patton was "not that income is broadly transferred from nonfarm people to farm people, but that such subsidies come from the general treasury, and that the funds in the treasury are principally collected by means of graduated income taxes. Thus, the transferred income in considerable degree is not transferred from 'nofarm people' but from the coffers of the wealthiest corporations in the country and from the better-off taxpayers." [95]

To Patton, the battle over production payments was fundamentally over a device which would promote more equitable redistribution of wealth. The facts as disclosed in this study, however, show clearly that whatever taxes well-to-do groups contributed toward maintaining the Brannan Plan would largely return to the more prosperous groups in agriculture.

For one reason or another, this paramount aspect of the Brannan Plan was almost wholly overlooked in the controversy over the Plan. Only a handful of agricultural economists, mainly at the University of Chicago, gave serious attention to this problem. So far as the politicians, the editorialists, the conservative critics, and the liberal champions of the Plan were concerned, the issue was almost ignored.

That a man with Brannan's background and unquestionably liberal inclinations should have chosen to devote his major energies as a Cabinet officer to a program which would primarily strengthen the economic position of relatively prosperous farmers is ironical. True, the Secretary later prepared and delivered some excellent Congressional testimony concerning measures to relieve poverty in agriculture.[96] But, as one of his intimates stated, the testimony was delivered and that was the end of it. There was no fight, no crusade, no nationwide public appeal.

Since agricultural economists generally agreed in 1950 (and agree today) that an effective program for dealing with poverty in agriculture is a crucial task of an enlightened farm policy, it is a pity that Brannan did not apply his considerable talents to the job, a job for which his training and liberal philosophy seemed to have fitted him so well.

Looking back upon the more legitimate criticisms leveled against the Brannan Plan, one is struck by their almost monotonous identification with the excessively high support standard. The attacks based on cost, on the possibility of reduced abundance, on the probability of spreading production controls, on the impact on foreign trade, and on the incidence of benefits all acquired strength or substance because of this standard. If the income support level had been reduced to a more realistic plane, the attractive features of the Plan would have received considerably more favorable attention than they got.

Certainly a cogent argument can be made for granting producers of certain perishable products equality of protection with producers of storables. Surely production payments have many advantages over price supports as a means of protecting farm income without penalizing consumers. A persuasive case can be made for requiring farmers receiving public funds to manage their soil in the public interest. There was much to be said for giving livestock producers preferential treatment in order to induce production shifts away from storables in chronic surplus. Reducing the massive subsidies to America's most prosperous farmers makes obvious sense.

One of the more politically astute of our agricultural economists, Walter W. Wilcox, has summarized the Brannan Plan as follows:

Of Secretary Brannan's six major proposals for change . . . in the light of my analysis and I believe in the light of recommendations of committees of The American Farm Economic Association, the first five are distinct improvements over existing legislation. . . . In common with almost all agricultural economists with whom I am acquainted, I have doubts about the desirability and feasibility of Secretary Brannan's high support standard. But I do not view this proposal with alarm. One doesn't need much political experience to conclude that there is little danger that price supports at too high a level will be adopted if direct government payments are used to implement any large part of them. The real danger is that Congress will not provide effective supports at any reasonable level for those products where direct payments are the only effective means of implementation. Congress simply will not appropriate the necessary funds.[97]

Dr. Wilcox' apprehensions concerning Congressional appropriations in support of a direct payment plan can not be lightly dismissed. But his warning is by no means conclusive evidence that the free market–direct payments principle might not provide the basis for a sounder agricultural policy than any amount of tinkering with a price support system.

It is probable, since the quite fantastic technological progress in U.S. farm production leads to a persistent overproduction of 4 to 8 per cent,[98] that a modified and enlarged soil bank is essential to a long-range solution of this part of the farm problem. If acreage controls and flexible price supports only reduce some surpluses at the price of creating others, an effective acreage retirement program may yet prove to be the only politically realistic answer to the overproduction dilemma.[99]

If such a program, then, were to relieve the production pressures which constantly depress farm prices and add billions to the agricultural budget, the free market–direct payments principle would become an increasingly attractive alternative to price supports. If direct payments were tied to a moderate income support level and *if no individual farmer was subsidized into an income bracket materially higher than that of the average urban working-class family,* the total cost to the taxpayer might well be both moderate and politically feasible. The gains to the consumer—farmer consumer and urban consumer alike— might also prove substantial, thereby making an important contribution to the problem of inflation control. Shucking the elaborate mechanism of government price supports and the inevitable headaches it entails would relieve the government of an enormous and difficult responsibility,[100] and would lead to a more rational use of our agricultural resources.

Even if an adequate soil bank were not adopted, the free market–direct payments proposal might be preferable to the current system (for some commodities, at least) if payments to individual farmers were limited to defensible levels. What possible justification can there be, anyway, for using tax money to raise farmers to an income plane above that of workers in industry? With the nation's farm population constantly shrinking, and farmers' political leverage declining accordingly, Congress ought to be asking this question with increasing frequency in the years ahead.

Be this as it may, Brannan's Plan might have been regarded as an example of genuine agricultural statesmanship, combining political shrewdness with a wholesome respect for the public interest, if the support standard alone had been modified to realistic levels. If so, why did not the debate center directly upon the level at which the support standard should be set? The nation was deluged with literature and oratory scoring the cost and the regimentation believed inherent in the Plan, but all too often these were attributed to production payments or to the nominal existence of extended controls, instead of to the support level. Why were not the sound features of the Plan salvaged, and its questionable support level trimmed to more acceptable levels?

The sensible attitude of the Rev. Shirley Greene, Agricultural Relations Secretary of the Council for Social Action, Congregational Christian Churches, was very nearly unique.[101] Said Rev. Greene: "We agree that Mr. Brannan probably set his goal too high. What would be wrong with operating the Brannan Plan machinery at lower and flexible support levels?" [102]

Unfortunately, the debate never moved onto a compromise plane. Instead, there was a doggedly irrational tendency on the part of most of Brannan's critics to look upon his proposals as unalterable, to be accepted or rejected *in toto*. The explanation of this phenomenon will be set forth in Chapter IV.

III

USDA INFORMATIONAL AND
PUBLICITY ACTIVITIES

Brannan's critics freely charged that the USDA engaged in an extravagant and probably illegal campaign to indoctrinate the American people with a favorable attitude toward the Brannan Plan. Typical of charges frequently brought against the Department was the statement by a Republican Congressman that "the USDA publicity machine has all stops out to win national support for the Brannan Plan." [1]

Let us examine and appraise the information and publicity activities of USDA relevant to the Brannan Plan during the period in which the latter was a prominent national issue—April 7, 1949, to November, 1950.

The Brannan Plan was a major news story from the day it was offered to Congress. The USDA, therefore, was immediately besieged with requests for information about it. Organization leaders, writers, and editors were eager to get the full story; ordinary citizens, too, wanted to find out more about it. It was evident that the Department would have to organize some method for handling the requests with which it was bombarded.

Department officials unanimously agree that there were no conferences to map out an informational strategy with which to "sell" the Plan to the people. Instead, a strictly stimuli-response situation developed, with activities emerging in piecemeal fashion as the needs appeared.

Two factors limited the freedom of the Department in what

must have been its instinctive desire to get its case before the public. The first was legal, the second political.

First, the Hatch Act permitted only six members of the Department to engage in "partisan activities" as defined by the Civil Service Commission.

Next, 18 U.S. Code 1913 (formerly 18 U.S. Code 201) stated: "No part of the money appropriated by any Act shall, in the absence of express authorization by Congress, be used directly or indirectly to pay for any personal service . . . telegram, telephone, letter, printed or written matter, or other device, intended or designed to influence in any manner a Member of Congress, to favor or oppose, by vote or otherwise any legislation or appropriation by Congress, whether before or after the introduction of any bill or resolution proposing such legislation . . ."

The phrase "to influence in any manner" is an ambiguous one. Since Congressmen pay heed to their constituents, this language could be interpreted as forbidding the distribution of any material to the general public written in such a manner as to predispose the reader to favor a given legislative solution to a public problem. According to Director of Information Robert L. Webster, this has in fact been the interpretation traditionally placed upon it by USDA.

The line between information and persuasion is a shadowy one, of course, with the former blending imperceptibly into the latter. More accurately, perhaps, all information is to some extent persuasive. While one could quibble endlessly about the distinctions between information and propaganda, it can not be disputed that if written material on a controversial matter is prepared with the understanding that "objectivity" is a legal requirement, the material will frequently have a different tone and content than if the writer does not operate under the same inhibitions.

For many years Congress has included the following language in the appropriation acts dealing with the Production and Marketing Administration: "Provided further, that none of the funds herein appropriated . . . shall be used to pay the salaries or expenses of any regional information employees or any State or county information employees, but this shall not preclude the answering of inquiries or supplying of information to individual farmers."

This section was the culmination of a bitter dispute in the North Central states between the Extension Service, backed by the Farm Bureau, and the Agricultural Adjustment Administration.[2] The latter had been accused of propagandizing on behalf of favored policies and against political candidates not of their choice. They were also charged with usurping educational functions properly belonging to the Extension Service.

The final restrictive statute was contained in 5 U.S. Code 54, which forbids the payment of salaries to publicity experts "unless specifically appropriated for that purpose."

Probably more important than the legal limitations (and the traditions which have grown out of them) in policing the informational work of the Department was the political atmosphere of the time. The traditional hostility between the executive and legislative branches of government had expressed itself, since the early days of the Roosevelt administration, in an increasingly heavy series of attacks upon the informational activities of the executive department.

It was repeatedly charged, by members of the opposition party, that vast numbers of open and concealed information officers within the executive establishment were debauching the people with enormous amounts of propaganda disguised as information. This propaganda was allegedly calculated to favorably impress the American people with the administration, the Democratic party, the programs being administered by the government, and with legislative proposals ardently desired by the "bureaucrats."

After the Democratic victory of 1936, John Hamilton, chairman of the Republican National Committee, issued a sharp statement in which he attributed his party's defeat in large part to propaganda emanating from the federal agencies during the preceding three years.[3]

In 1937 Brookings Institute undertook a study for the Select

Committee to Investigate Executive Agencies of the Government. The report of the Select Committee, based on this study, estimated that federal publicity and "propaganda" were costing the government $1,200,000 per year.[4]

Attacks upon the propaganda activities of the federal government gained momentum as Democratic executive tenure lengthened. A few quotations from the late war and postwar period may help to reveal the intensity of feeling which had developed over the years among members of the opposition party. Senator Taft declared: "Propaganda, particularly propaganda backed by the unlimited force of government funds, is likely to destroy democracy from within. I welcome factual information from the Government, even that which argues openly for Administration policies, if it gives a reasonable statement of the position of its opponents. I object to the misrepresentation contained in the present propaganda, to the smearing of opponents, to stirring up pressure groups against Congress."[5]

John Taber, economy-minded senior Republican member of the House Appropriations Committee, was also quoted as saying that "the activities of the so-called publicity bureaus are a menace to decent government. Our people are being forced to pay for propaganda which is destroying their own liberties."[6] Former Senator George A. Wilson commented, "Some of these government bureaus are among the most vicious propagandists of this generation."[7]

The first formal investigation of alleged executive propaganda took place in 1946.[8] The Harness Subcommittee on Publicity and Propaganda of the Committee on Expenditures in the Executive Departments investigated five legislative fields, one being agriculture. The Committee adjudged that unlawful propaganda activities had been committed in each area. The probe into agriculture involved charges that county committee chairmen of PMA had been pressured by state PMA officials to protest an impending Congressional slash in the appropriations for the Agricultural Conservation Payments program administered by PMA.

The Committee report concluded, "The evidence shows that

. . . Government funds were used in an improper manner for propaganda activities supporting attempts to restore to the budget cuts in appropriations as voted by the House of Representatives." [9] Although a minority of the Committee took exception to the majority findings, the important point for our purposes is that the investigation and the findings were made.

The report of the Committee led to allegations such as this: "On the home front, the Department of Agriculture is by far the most prolific vendor of official propaganda. In that Department . . . investigators found 525 persons engaged in public relations work." [10]

Under the prevailing circumstances, it was only natural that the Department of Agriculture should tread warily in the course of its informational work. With both "publicity officers" and the Department under sharp attack and close scrutiny, prudence would dictate a conservative course of action.

USDA had a number of avenues open to it in presenting its case to the people. The Secretary and certain of his assistants could make speeches. These could be issued as press releases and distributed to its far-flung state and local units, to the press services, and to other groups and persons. Requests for information could be filled. Articles on the Plan could be written for magazines wishing this service. Letters of protest and commendation could be written to newspapers and magazines discussing the Plan. Finally, top Department officials could co-operate with the Democratic party in its campaign to explain and foster the Plan. All of these media were used by the Department in the course of the next eighteen months.

In using the term "Department" some clarification is in order. The initiative in all of the information and publicity work cited above (except for the processing of press releases and the answering of requests for information) came from the Secretary and his immediate assistants, not from the Office of Information. The latter operated in response to specific instructions from the Secretary's Office or in conformity with long-standing practice. For example, the Secretary's speeches concerning his Plan were not released merely as a means of publicizing the Plan. Speeches by the Secretary of Agriculture are automatically issued as press releases in accordance with a practice long antedating Brannan's appointment to that post.

The organization of information and publicity work in the Department was as follows: The Office of Information answered correspondence on the Plan, processed and distributed press releases, and handled Department publications going to USDA employees, to radio farm directors, and to farm papers. It also worked up the script for the Department radio programs. The various bureaus had information offices of their own which handled such bureau organs as *Rural Electrification News, Soil Conservation*, etc.

The Secretary himself decided what materials should be available for public distribution. He was also obliged to personally receive those desiring information whose prestige or position demanded this courtesy. John Baker and Wesley McCune were detailed to discuss the Plan with journalists and writers who wanted full information on it, and with others who had no special claim on the Secretary's time.

President Truman reported at a press conference on September 18, 1949, that he had asked the Secretary to conduct a speech-making campaign on behalf of the Brannan Plan. A Secretary of Agriculture, of course, makes many speeches during the course of even a relatively untroubled administrative tenure, and the President's decision swelled the Secretary's speaking load. Between April 7, 1949, and November, 1950, Brannan made 126 major speeches. In seventy-eight of these, he devoted some time to discussing his Plan or some of its features. These speeches carried him into twenty-five states and the District of Columbia, and included appearances on ten major network broadcasts. An estimated 30 to 40 speeches on the Plan were also made by Brannan's staff.

A large proportion of the information work done by the Department derived from the speeches and Congressional testimony delivered by Brannan himself. His opening testimony on April 7, 1949; his testimony on April 25, 1949, dealing with the cost of the Plan; and his speech, "Fact vs. Fantasy," delivered before the Ohio Farm Committee at Columbus, Ohio, on March 28, 1950—all were widely circulated. In addition, almost 75 per cent of the press releases which dealt in whole or in part with the Brannan Plan recorded speeches made by the Secretary.

We can get some idea of the informational role of USDA by noting the quantity of literature which it issued explaining or promoting the Plan, in whole or in part. The Department issued approximately 4,650 press releases from April 7, 1949, to November 7, 1950. Of these, fifty were concerned, to some extent, with explanation and/or advocacy of the Brannan Plan. This adds up to slightly over 1 per cent of the total number of releases issued during this period.

Examined from another position, these 4,650 press releases contained approximately 10,500 pages of printed matter. Of this total, about 340 pages dealt with the Brannan Plan or with one or more of its principal features. Thus slightly over 3 per cent of the total number of press release pages during this eighteen-month period was devoted to publicizing the Brannan Plan. Since an average of 1,000 copies were made and distributed on each of these press releases, this would mean that roughly 50,000 pieces of informational material on the Brannan Plan were issued via this medium.

The Department ordered and distributed 28,000 copies of the Secretary's April 7, 1949, testimony; 13,000 copies of his testimony before the Senate and House Agricultural Committees on April 25, 1949; 2,500 copies of the speech, "Fact vs. Fantasy"; and 7,600 copies of "Questions and Answers" (the latter was prepared by the Department to answer specific questions which had been raised about the operation of the Plan, and to correct certain misimpressions which the Department believed were being created).

The Report of the Secretary of Agriculture for 1949 contained several pages pleading the case for production payments as an alternative to price supports for perishables. About 5,000 copies of this document were printed and distributed.

A few other items concerning the Brannan Plan were prepared by the Department for distribution to interested persons.

About 500 copies of a two-page explanation of "Essential Parts in Administration Price Support Proposal" were printed. Although no records are available, it is estimated that between 500 and 1,000 copies of "Comparison of the Price Support Provisions of the Agricultural Act of 1948 with Changes Recommended by the U.S. Department of Agriculture" were printed. A similar printing was made of a document comparing the Brannan Plan with the Agricultural Act of 1949.

Finally, some 250,000 copies of the *Agricultural Situation,* containing about four pages summarizing the Brannan Plan, were printed and distributed by the Department.

In summary, something over 355,000 pieces of informational material dealing with the Brannan Plan were issued by the Department for general and departmental use during this eighteen-month period. To keep this fact in focus, however, it must be emphasized that not all of the fifty press releases mentioned above were wholly devoted to the Plan. In some instances only a page or two of a fifteen-page release may have dwelt on the Plan. Only two of 136 pages of the Secretary's annual report discussed the need for production payments. And only a fraction of the *Agricultural Situation* described the Plan. The latter publication, incidentally, is issued monthly, and contained no further reference to Brannan's proposals.

The preceding account, however, does not represent the total extent of Department informational work along these lines. A special article was written for *Sperryscope,* entitled "Partners in Prosperity." Another, "This Is My Proposal," went to *Southern Planter.* "A Program for the Whole People," was prepared and sent to *America.* Other articles went to *Consumers on the March* and to *The Breeder's Gazette.* Members of the Secretary's staff indicate that other articles may have been written for which no records exist.

After an early burst of inquiries, a surprisingly small number of written requests for material on the Plan came into the Department. Only 825 letters and postcards are on file asking for such material. Of these, about 300 are from students or members of the academic profession.

Some of the letters asked for comparatively large quantities of informational matter. For example, the *California Farm Reporter* requested 1,000 copies of Brannan Plan material; the Farmers Union Livestock Commission of South Dakota and the United Packinghouse Workers (CIO) of Des Moines, Iowa, similarly called for 1,000 copies. Several Democratic party organizations asked for hundreds of copies. In each instance cited, the requests were filled.

At first, only the Secretary's original Congressional testimony was mailed to those asking for information. After the question of cost became a major issue, Brannan's testimony on April 25, 1949, was added. "Questions and Answers," drawn up in May, 1949, was next added to the "Brannan Kit." Finally, the speech, "Fact vs. Fantasy," formed the fourth and last item furnished by the Office of Information.

To keep the cost within the funds allocated for informational purposes by the Congress, reprints of material inserted in the *Congressional Record* were freely used. The first three items in the "Brannan Kit" were inserted in the *Record,* and used in reprint form by the Department. This cut printing costs almost in half.

Whom did this material reach? Over 13,000 copies of Brannan's initial Congressional testimony went to USDA agencies, 4,000 going to the Production and Marketing Administration, 2,000 to the Rural Electrification Administration, 1,265 to the Secretary's Office, and 700 to the Extension Service.

Several hundred copies were used by the press services in Washington, and approximately 400 copies went to editors of farm papers. Another 250 copies were mailed to radio stations which carry special farm features. Over 150 copies were circulated to what is known as the "Secretary's list"—a group of persons who have asked to receive copies of every speech or policy statement made by the Secretary. In some instances these persons have an official interest in the Secretary's pronouncements and in others only a general interest.

Finally, copies went to the major farm organizations, the various commodity organizations, the Democratic and Republican national committees, and numerous nonfarm organizations who had asked to be put on the mailing list for important Department releases.

The distribution of the testimony presented to Congress on April 25, 1949, could not be determined. Records were not available, although the mimeographing of 3,000 copies for original distribution indicates that a fairly extensive distribution was made.

"Questions and Answers" received much the same distributional treatment as the testimony of April 7, 1949, with a few exceptions. As for "Fact vs. Fantasy," distribution data again proved inadequate.

A number of press releases recording speeches on the Plan were checked in an effort to obtain a typical picture of the distribution of the fifty releases referred to earlier. From 1,000 to 1,200 copies were run off on each of three releases. The fourth, which appears to have been of more than average importance, consisted of 2,100 copies. Besides the usual distribution to the press services, to those on the "Secretary's list," and to Department units receiving all releases, distribution was made in each case to PMA state committees and to state extension directors. In no instance did releases go to other field offices within the Department.

Additional distribution of these releases was made as follows: in the case of a speech by Assistant Secretary Knox Hutchinson before the National Poultry, Butter and Egg Association, copies were mailed to livestock papers, dairy papers, and poultry papers; the Secretary's speech at the National Farm Institute went to educational magazines, state commissioners of agriculture, farm papers, farm organization papers, radio farm program directors, co-operative papers, and to a list of free lance writers who have asked for certain types of releases; Brannan's speech before the Ohio State Grange was distributed to farm papers, radio farm program directors, and state commissioners of agriculture; and a speech at Juneau, Wisconsin, went only to dairy papers (in addition to the general distribution referred to above).

Since speeches similar to those cited were made before many different groups, with each speech slanted somewhat differently to meet the supposed interests of the various groups, press release material on the Brannan Plan eventually fanned out to a relatively wide number of papers, organizations, and persons interested in agricultural policy.

Information on the Brannan Plan reached more people, directly, through an article by Wesley McCune in the *Agricultural Situation*, than by any other single medium. This paper is distributed to about 250,000 persons, mostly crop reporters. By reaching this group, in addition to the 3,000 county PMA committees, the Department was able to bring the facts, as it saw them, to the attention of an imposing number of leading farmers throughout the nation.

A comparatively insignificant amount of information went out to field officers of the Department of Agriculture via the regular agency publications. For example, the *Extension Service Review*, a monthly issued by the Extension Service to workers and co-operators of USDA who were engaged in extension activities, contained virtually no material descriptive of the Brannan Plan. Neither did *Soil Conservation*, which goes to a small number of workers and official co-operators of the Department engaged in soil-conservation activities, and to libraries, agricultural colleges, experiment stations, and similar institutions. *Rural Electrification News*, published by REA; *Agricultural Economics Research*, by BAE; *News for Farmer Cooperatives* by Farm Credit Administration; and the *PMA Daily Bulletin* (distributed to state PMA committees) all were devoid of information on the Plan. Farmers Home Administration memoranda to state directors, however, included copies of the April 7, 1949, testimony and "Questions and Answers," plus the April 25, 1949, testimony on cost, and the Secretary's speech before the National Farmers Union annual convention at Denver, Colorado, on March 6, 1950.

The Department was circumspect in handling its regular radio programs over the major networks. The National Farm and Home Hour on April 9, 1949, carried some remarks by the

Secretary about his Plan. The only other reference to the Brannan Plan occurred on May 7, 1949, when the Secretary very briefly explained how cotton would be affected by his proposals. "The American Farmer," an American Broadcasting Company program, contained two brief references to the Brannan Plan which occupied a total of perhaps ten minutes of radio time. The "Columbia Country Journal," a Columbia Broadcasting System five-minute short feature (discontinued after July 16, 1949), contained no descriptive material on the Plan.

The above statements apply to regular Department programs. The Secretary and members of his staff, of course, took part in many other radio programs at the invitation of radio program directors or interested groups, but not on time donated to the Department by the networks.

A final, if relatively unimportant, method was employed for reaching the general public. Brannan wrote an occasional letter to newspapers or magazines which had given either a favorable or unfavorable twist to its description or analysis of the Plan. Since he was the Secretary of Agriculture, his letters to the editor would receive publication priority, thus enabling him to counter adverse publicity to a small extent.

It would, of course, be possible for the Department to encourage friendly organizations to publicize the Brannan Plan, or to collaborate with them on informational work. However, the National Farmers Union, Americans for Democratic Action, CIO Political Action Committee, United Automobile Workers, Labor's League for Political Education, and Public Affairs Institute were all interviewed with regard to possible collaboration and liaison with the Department in preparing speeches or written matter, organizing meetings, etc.[11] Without exception, it was reported that the total relationship with the Department was confined to: (1) receipt, by these organizations, of materials on the Plan which would normally reach them because of standing requests, or because of a specific request, for information; (2) departmental checking, upon request, of the accuracy of factual material on the Plan which these organizations were preparing to issue.

It is reasonable to assume that members of the Secretary's staff offered some suggestions to improve the effectiveness of material submitted for their appraisal, but this remains no more than conjectural. At any rate, no evidence whatever was found to indicate that the Department took the initiative in urging other organizations to carry the ball for it.

INFORMATIONAL ACTIVITIES OF THE EXTENSION SERVICE

The USDA Extension Service, since it has connections with county agents in practically all of our 3,050 counties, offers an interesting study in the informational opportunities and practices of the Department. The county agents, jointly supervised by USDA and the state colleges, are officially vested with responsibility for carrying out field informational work among the farmers.

Copies of the Secretary's original testimony, his subsequent testimony on cost, "Questions and Answers," and each of the fifty press releases on the Brannan Plan were sent to state extension directors and editors. As a general rule, directors prepared either a summary of the Secretary's testimony or, with the assistance of a state extension economist, other material explaining the operation of the Plan and comparing it with other proposals. Occasionally this was supplemented by appraisals of the Plan prepared by leading farm organizations or prominent agricultural experts. This material was then sent directly to county agents.[12]

In some instances, however, directors availed themselves of the offer by the Washington office to supply, upon request, additional copies of important material. Some directors called for and received sufficient copies of several USDA documents to supply each county agent within the state. At least one director sent copies of the April 7 testimony not only to county agents but to home demonstration agents and women specialists also. Generally, however, it appears that state directors did not obtain copies for county-wide distribution. It was entirely within their discretion to do as they pleased in this matter.

For many years county agents have been briefed on important

agricultural issues at district meetings. These meetings, therefore, served as a medium for acquainting agents with factual
aspects of the Plan, as well as with alternative proposals currently receiving attention. Some extension personnel on both
state and local levels also took part in public forums or other
meetings discussing the Brannan Plan. In many cases they
served as moderators, explaining the mechanics of the Plan and
then stepping aside for other speakers to present the pros and
cons.

The extension director of a state which had carried on an
especially active informational program on public policy matters wrote, "Four hundred ten meetings were held under the
County Agricultural Agents' direction where State-staff members participated in public policy discussions. A total of 57,650
people were in attendance. Many of these were leader-meetings
with groups ranging from 10 to 40 people." [13]

Another director commented: "We have used a team of two
specialists, one a sociologist, the other a planning specialist who
has an Agricultural Economics background. One of the specialists handled the social aspects and background of government
activities. The other followed out a factual presentation. We
used different agricultural programs and drew factual comparisons between them."

This practice applied to public policy discussions in general,
not merely to discussions of the Brannan Plan.

An interesting consultative and administrative device was
used in another state for meeting its informational responsibilities in this field. The director writes:

Soon after the Brannan Plan was proposed we had a conference
with the leaders of the Farm Bureau, Grange, PMA, FHA, Agricultural Extension, and others to discuss what should be done in our
state to inform our people about the Brannan Plan and other price
support programs. It was proposed that a series of district meetings be
held in the state for all leaders. The Farm Bureau was very interested
in working on the Brannan Plan and in getting some opinions from
their people concerning it. It was agreed that the Farm Bureau would
sponsor district meetings throughout the state and that the other

agencies would co-operate on the project. All agencies agreed to participate as long as the meetings were not set for making decisions or registering votes on the Plan. Extension agreed to co-operate by appearing on the program to discuss the pros and cons of the Plan.

The state extension services provided publicity on the Brannan Plan in other ways also. A typical statement from one director reads: "A series of news releases analyzing various features of the Brannan Plan were prepared by the head of our Department of Agricultural Economics and these were released by the Extension Service to the press and radio."

A state supervisor for co-operative programs stated, "It has been our policy not to initiate promotion or propaganda[!] regarding any proposed program until Congress has adopted such program." [14] He added: "A circular letter was sent to the county agricultural agents, urging them to take part as ex-officio members of the county PMA committees in holding county-wide meetings to discuss the features of the Brannan Plan." [15]

In at least one instance, a regional conference of extension directors was addressed by a USDA official (in this case, O. V. Wells) on the subject of the Brannan Plan. The director reporting this incident declared: "Mr. Wells stated that staff members of the USDA had been told by Secretary Brannan that they were not expected to be proponents of the Plan but should be able to explain its provisions. This was the attitude of Mr. Wells at this meeting."

The conference referred to, it should be mentioned, was a routine affair and had not been called for the purpose of acquainting members with the Brannan Plan.

INFORMATIONAL ACTIVITIES OF PMA

As the most powerful organizational unit within the Department of Agriculture and one with a far-flung local organizational base, PMA's informational and publicity activities in the area of this study were of special interest. PMA administered the system of acreage allotments, marketing quotas, and the loan and purchase agreement program whereby the price-support system for storable commodities was maintained. In addition—and this became the principal work of local PMA committees during peacetime years when allotments and quotas were not in general operation—it administered the Agricultural Conservation Payments program, whereby co-operating farmers received some $250,000,000 annually for carrying out soil conservation or soil-building practices.

On the local operational level PMA's responsibilities were met by locally elected county committees. About 9,085 county committeemen and 85,400 community committeemen administered the program in what the Department of Agriculture proudly referred to as grass-roots democracy at work.

Numerous charges have been made that the PMA organization had become, in some sense, an adjunct of the Democratic party. For example, Professor Hardin writes:

In some PMA meetings after the 1948 election, there was a disposition to claim credit for a share in President Truman's victory. PMA committeemen were much in evidence at the midwestern Democratic rally in Des Moines, May, 1949.

Promotions from county committees to the state PMA committee in one midwestern state, at least, were based not only upon one's Democratic regularity but upon one's belonging to the right faction in the Democratic party—according to the declarations of a number of persons to the writer in 1948–1950.[16]

Hardin observes further, "The network of state, county and community committeemen constitutes an information service with great possibilities of indoctrination with respect to farmers' attitudes and opinions."[17]

Ralph S. Trigg, director of PMA, made it clear at an early date that he was not going to use PMA as a medium for propagandizing for the Brannan Plan. AAA (from which PMA emerged in the reorganization of 1945) had been subjected to severe criticism for allegedly engaging in partisan activities during the war, with state and regional PMA information offices casualties of the political infighting.[18] Upon assuming the directorship of PMA, Trigg assured interested Congressmen that there would be no repetition, if he could help it, of the wartime political maneuvers.

So far as could be determined, there is no evidence that Trigg or his immediate assistants deviated from the neutral position officially adopted. Trigg appears to have bent over backward to avoid the shadow of suspicion. Although he made a number of speeches during the period in which the Brannan Plan was making news, he carefully avoided making references to it, or to the principles it contained. As a result, criticism of PMA "propaganda" on behalf of the Brannan Plan largely bypassed the agency's top-level Washington officials.

Secretary Brannan apparently concurred in PMA's policy of neutrality toward his Plan. According to both Trigg and Woolley, the Secretary at no time suggested to them—directly or by inference—that PMA's organizational network should be used to churn up sentiment for the Brannan Plan.[19] Brannan's official position on informational work by Departmental field personnel was stated on several occasions—once before an annual PMA conference, and once before a similar conference of extension directors. The Secretary said he did not ask Department members to support the Plan. He asked only that those in positions exposing themselves to public inquiries understand it and be prepared to answer questions accurately about it.

When "Questions and Answers" was prepared and readied for distribution, Trigg decided the answers to the first fifteen questions bore a somewhat propagandistic flavor. To play safe, Trigg drafted a letter of transmittal for copies of "Questions and Answers" going to state committees, which read in part as follows: "If requests from farmers for factual information would make it advisable, you may wish to send your county committees excerpts from the sections on 'General Mechanics of Program Operation' which begin on page five. I do not think that distribution of the full "Questions and Answers" statement, beyond the State Offices, is needed at this time."[20]

Whether the Secretary knew about or was pleased with this decision is not known. At any rate, he did not seek to overrule Trigg.[21]

Numerous charges were made that state and county PMA personnel worked to create an affirmative attitude towards the Brannan Plan. An article in *Fortune,* for example, reported: "The PMA state fieldmen travel around in automobiles and drop in to visit farmers. As government employees they are not allowed to politick, but they are expected to 'answer questions' about any USDA program—notably, at present, the Brannan Plan. Throughout the Middle West this kind of indoctrination by PMA fieldmen is known with a wink as 'pasture breeding.' " [22]

Substantiation or refutation of these and many similar charges is extremely difficult to establish. There is agreement by informed persons, however, that PMA officials in some Midwest and North Central states were more actively engaged in informational work than were comparable officials in other states. There is also agreement that PMA officials in some states took a completely unexceptionable position. So far as actual violation of law is concerned, Professor Hardin says: "Research has found no examples of PMA officials found guilty of violations of the Hatch Act or of departmental regulations." [23]

On the basis of questionnaires submitted to all of the chairmen of state PMA committees, certain observations can be made concerning PMA informational activities on the state and local levels in connection with the Brannan Plan. These observations do not, of course, make any distinction between informational and propaganda activities. Obviously, PMA people were not going to voluntarily admit to propaganda activities of any kind. It also may be taken for granted that some respondents failed to divulge all of the strictly informational activities in which they took part. Generalizations of any kind derived from data assembled in this manner must therefore be limited and severely qualified. A number of the thirty-five replies, however, did shed light on the character of PMA informational work in this area.

The overwhelming majority of respondents indicated that the Secretary's testimony of April 7, 1949, circulated down to state PMA fieldmen and the local PMA county committees. A considerable number of chairmen stated that the Secretary's subsequent testimony on April 25 also was passed on to the counties. The same applies to "Questions and Answers." In the case of the latter, all forty-six questions were reproduced in most cases, not merely the last thirty-one questions dealing with the actual mechanics of the Plan as had been suggested by the Washington PMA office.

A few state committees acknowledged that they had prepared and mailed to the local committees additional material explaining the functioning of the Brannan Plan. One state sent each county committee a "Suggested Radio Script" describing the Brannan Plan in highly favorable language, and ending: "Friends, you have been listening to a public interest broad- cast . . ." The same state committee distributed to its fieldmen a pamphlet prepared by the Farmers Union entitled, "We're Going Down the Sliding Scale." This pamphlet frankly extolled the Brannan Plan and attacked the "sliding scale."

A newsletter distributed by another state committee to county and community committeemen notified them that Brannan would discuss his farm plan at an open meeting in a city within the state. The newsletter read as follows: "Here is a chance to get all the facts straight from Secretary Brannan on his 'farm plan.' Come early and be here for the 9 A.M. conference meet- ing. . . . Let folks in your county know about this important meeting."

It is apparent from replies to the questionnaire that discus- sion of the Brannan Plan took place at one time or another at almost all district or county meetings. In some instances state committeemen explained the Plan to county committeemen; in others, fieldmen led discussion on the subject. Many chairmen said that field men confined themselves to answering questions raised by members of the county committees. Some state com- mitteemen spoke on the Plan before farm organizations or civic groups. One member admitted taking the pro side in several public debates on the Brannan Plan.[24] Other state committee- men said they discussed the Plan on radio programs. A number of chairmen acknowledged that materials on the Plan were

available in their offices to give to persons desiring information
on it.[25]

It is clear that there was a wide variation in the amount of
informational work on the Brannan Plan done by the various
state committees. Some were at least as active as the law allowed,
while others claim to have confined their efforts to distributing
to county committees copies of the Secretary's opening testimony. Under the circumstances, it is difficult to generalize beyond this point.

THE "CAPTIVE AUDIENCE" AT ST. PAUL

One of the more interesting chapters in the publicity work of
the Department of Agriculture took place in connection with
the annual meeting of the Minnesota Committeemen of the
Production and Marketing Administration on April 3 and 4,
1950. A study of this meeting well illustrated the propaganda
potentialities of the PMA committee system, as well as the great
difficulties involved in establishing legal safeguards to curb government propaganda.

On March 16, 1950, Charles W. Stickney, chairman of the
Minnesota State PMA Committee, notified the 4,254 community
committeemen (who help county committeemen administer the
PMA program) as follows:

The state committee has arranged for you to attend the 2nd day
of the annual Minnesota County PMA Committee meeting in the
arena of the St. Paul Auditorium on Tuesday, April 4.
The decline in farm prices has placed even greater emphasis on the
price-support program which we in PMA are administering. We know
you realize how controversial this subject has become. We feel it is
extremely important for you community committeemen who represent agriculture at the grass roots to have this chance to hear your
Secretary who is making a terrific fight to maintain some measure of
economic stability for farmers. . . . We feel sure that giving you an
opportunity to hear your Administrator on this subject will give you
renewed enthusiasm and a broader understanding of the problems
which now confront us.[26]

The letter noted that mileage allowance was authorized and that a "regular day's pay" would be received for attending the meeting. Another letter was sent to the 267 county committeemen, inviting their attendance at St. Paul for *both* April 3 and 4, 1950. Senators Edward J. Thye (R–Minn.) and Hubert H. Humphrey (D–Minn.) were invited to address the convention on April 4. Dewey Anderson, Director of Public Affairs Institute, was also invited to speak on the same date. The main attraction, however, was to be Brannan himself.

Approximately 2,077 community committeemen and 245 county committeemen, plus ten USDA officials and an undetermined number of other persons attended the meeting, which had been widely publicized as an "open" meeting. The program distributed in the auditorium carried a message on the back entitled, "Lest We Forget," listing grain prices for December 24, 1932, and adding: "It could happen again." [27] This message had been prepared by the state PMA committee.

Republican Senator Thye was unable to attend the meeting, thus leaving the field open—so far as the discussion of domestic agricultural policy was concerned—to Senator Humphrey and Secretary Brannan. Both gentlemen proceeded to unlimber their heaviest artillery. Humphrey delivered a biting attack on the Aiken Act and on the philosophy of flexible supports, and stoutly defended the Brannan Plan. Brannan discoursed with animation and eloquence on the virtues of his Plan and on the evil tactics of its (and his) enemies.[28]

Alfred D. Stedman, former Information Director and Assistant Administrator of AAA, reporting the meeting for the *St. Paul Dispatch,* wrote: "A new nation-wide fight for the Brannan farm plan, with no quarter asked or given, was launched for the Truman administration by Secretary of Agriculture Brannan in St. Paul today." [29] A considerable hue and cry was promptly raised in Minnesota papers to the effect that the Department had organized a "captive audience," financed by public funds, for the purpose of advancing the political interests of Brannan and the Truman administration.

On April 11, 1950, Senator George D. Aiken, speaking in the

Senate, called Secretary Brannan to task. [30] Asserting that the community committeemen were "virtually instructed to appear at the St. Paul meeting," he charged that the meeting must have cost between $50,000 and $100,000.[31] This money, he said, must have come from "federal funds allocated to Minnesota for soil-improvement work." He continued:

I have searched diligently through the transcript of the full speech made by Secretary Brannan at St. Paul and can find nowhere that he makes any reference to the subject matter for which the conference of county committeemen was called, namely, the formulating and administration of agricultural programs as authorized by law. . . . The speeches of both the Secretary and the junior Senator from Minnesota were political from start to finish, and money appropriated to the D. A. for soil-conservation purposes cannot be legally spent in hiring audiences for political purposes. . . . I know of no authority which permits the Comptroller General to approve the expenditure of PMA funds for the purpose of [sic] which they were used at St. Paul. . . . When I see attempts made with the use of Federal funds appropriated for other purposes to discredit the acts of Congress, then I wonder how long we will tolerate an attitude which regards the work of a legislative body elected by the people as a detriment to good administration.[32]

Senator Aiken then sent a letter to the Comptroller General, Lindsay Warren, calling for a ruling on the legality of the expenditures involved in the meeting. Warren, in turn, asked Secretary Brannan for a report on the meeting.

Brannan's reply [33] stressed the fact that attendance at the meeting of community committeemen would not be a burden on the taxpayer. Congress, he said, appropriated a given amount of money to pay for the services of community committeemen; when this sum was exhausted, committeemen continued to work without compensation. Brannan further pointed out that Senator Aiken himself spoke at the Vermont State PMA Conference in 1949. "Each of the two preceding Secretaries of Agriculture had spoken at an identical type of meeting" and Secretary of Agriculture Clinton P. Anderson, in 1948, discussed "existing

and proposed farm legislation." Brannan denied that he himself
had mentioned political parties or political candidates during
his speech. He insisted that "there is nothing about the con-
vening or conduct of this meeting which is in anywise different
from many other meetings which have been held this year and
in previous years throughout the country by this and many other
agencies of Government."

As for the charge of impropriety concerning the invitation
to, and payment of, community committeemen, the Secretary
argued: "Community committeemen and county committeemen
are engaged in the very same type of program and therefore if,
as is already acknowledged, this meeting was perfectly proper
as far as county committeemen are concerned, it very logically
follows that it was equally proper as far as community committeemen are concerned."

Following his investigations, Comptroller General Warren
wrote Senator Aiken that PMA was authorized to provide for
meetings "when necessary to the successful administration of
the program . . . the said salary and expenses appear to constitute administrative expenses incurred by the county committeemen in cooperating in the carrying out of the program which
the Secretary of Agriculture . . . is authorized and directed to
pay out of funds made available for such programs. The meeting considered as a whole appears to have familiarized such
committeemen with the workings of the program, and it is believed that the salary and expenses of the community committeemen are properly authorized to be paid as administrative expenses of the county committeemen." [34]

In discussing the Comptroller General's letter on the Senate
floor, Senator Aiken first observed that Warren expressly denied
drawing any conclusions concerning a possible violation of
18 U.S. Code, 1913, pointing out that enforcement of this provision was a responsibility of the Justice Department. He then
proceeded to take sharp exception to the Comptroller General's ruling.

The crux of the matter, he said, is whether "expenses and
salaries of community committeemen could be paid in connec-

tion with their attendance at the second day of the St. Paul meeting for the purpose of hearing political speeches." He noted: "Community committeemen were not even invited to attend the first day of the meeting on April 3 which was publicized by the PMA as the day on which county committeemen would 'make plans for the year's conservation work. . . .' I cannot see how you can justify paying community committeemen for attending the second day of the St. Paul meeting on the ground that community committeemen can attend meetings 'when necessary to the successful administration of the program.' I don't see how even Secretary Brannan's discussion of the proposed Brannan Plan has anything to do with the successful administration of the program now on the statute books, which is the only program community or county committeemen have any responsibility for administering."

Referring to Warren's statement that "the salary and expenses of the community committeemen who assist the county committees in carrying out the program appear properly to be for consideration as an administrative expense of the county committee," he remarked sarcastically that "according to this interpretation the county committee can hire anyone to attend any meeting for any purpose."

Warren's reply to Aiken's second letter [35] stressed the fact that his decision dealt only with "the bare legal question involved—the availability of appropriations for the payments to community committeemen. . . . That does not necessarily mean, of course, that I approve the meeting or the way in which it was conducted. As you know, I have no authority to disallow or withhold credits for payments because they may have been made extravagantly or unwisely."

With reference to 18 U.S. Code, 1913, he again pointed out that this was not within his power to enforce. Should judicial action be instituted, he added, "It probably would afford no basis for disallowing credit for the payments made to the community committeemen. They were paid for attending the meeting and not for attempting to influence anyone."

The St. Paul episode involved four major questions. (1) Was

the government legally obligated to pay travel expenses and per diem for community committeemen under the circumstances surrounding the meeting on April 4? (2) Was Secretary Brannan's speech in violation of 18 U.S. Code, 1913? (3) Was it ethically proper to invite community committeemen to a meeting at which political speeches were paramount, and administrative instruction secondary? (4) Was it ethically proper for the Secretary to take advantage of this opportunity to peddle his favorite agricultural gospel?

The first question appears to have been unequivocally settled by a disclosure, during the course of the hearings of the House Select Committee on Lobbying Activities, that PMA Deputy Administrator Frank Woolley and PMA State Chairman Charles Stickney did devote some time during the morning session of the April 4 meeting to discussing administrative problems relevant to the duties of PMA county and community committeemen. Whether or not the Comptroller General was aware of this is not known. If he were, it is difficult to account for his failure to directly mention the point in his correspondence with Senator Aiken, although his statement that "the meeting considered as a whole appears to have familiarized such committeemen with the workings of the program" may have reflected his knowledge of the fact.

At any rate, in view of Senator Aiken's failure to lodge any protest against payment to the county committeemen, there would have been no questioning the legal obligation to make payments to community committeemen if Stickney's and Woolley's role had been directly emphasized. Warren's observation that committeemen were paid for "attending the meeting and not for attempting to influence anyone" apparently settles the point that, regardless of 18 U.S. Code, 1913, the payments were legally proper.

Some Congressmen contended that it was improper for Department officials to "run around the country" making political speeches or advocating pet legislative proposals at the taxpayers' expense. Such activity, they argued, was contrary to law. Cabinet officers, of course, have been making political speeches at the taxpayers' expense since the days of Hamilton and Jefferson, as the Congressmen must have known. This practice is warmly defended by those taking a broad view of the leadership role of the Chief Executive.[36]

That formidable difficulties are associated with any attempt to employ 18 U.S. Code, 1913, in an effort to restrain administrative officials from political activities was made abundantly clear by representatives of the General Accounting Office at the hearings before the House Select Committee on Lobbying Activities. Frank H. Weitzel, Assistant to the Comptroller General, reported:

In many cases it is obviously hard, if not impossible, to recognize the unlawful use of federal funds for lobbying activities from documents submitted with the account to the GAO. . . . For example, a trip of a Government official to Washington might in fact have been intended and directed because of the official's capacity to enlist the aid of a certain Member or Members of Congress in legislation of interest to the department. The vouchers for the reimbursement of travel expenses covering such a trip will very seldom reveal the true purpose of the trip, which is usually described as being "for official business." [37]

Another and greater difficulty was also pointed out.

I think it is the law that an officer of the Government, as distinguished from an employee, earns his salary by virtue of his status, in other words, through holding his commission rather than through performance of detailed duties. So, if he performs some official duties on a trip and at night has to make a speech and his travel expenses are paid by the Government, it is extremely difficult or even impossible, frankly, to segregate the official from what you might call the political.[38]

Even assuming that a decision was made that a given expenditure was illegal, a further disability exists. The Comptroller General does not make a practice of independently withholding funds on the grounds that their expenditure violated 18 U.S.

Code, 1913. Charles Johnson, testifying for the Comptroller General, declared:

> The Comptroller General from his experience realizes that if a determination is made [that] there is a legal liability to the U.S., there would be possibly an imputation of a concomitant criminal liability. There would be a tendency toward the establishment of a prima facie case where the GAO made a disallowance of an expense payment and the matter was subject to judicial determination. . . . Under those circumstances it has always been the policy of the GAO to go further and report all of the facts to the Attorney General for such action as he deems necessary under the criminal portion of the statute.

Johnson added, significantly: "I don't know personally of a single instance in which we have had a judicial determination upholding our finding that an illegal expenditure was made under this statute. I have made a brief search for it." [39]

Several observations should be made in connection with the question of whether the Minnesota State PMA Committee invitation to the community committeemen was in accordance with sound political and administrative ethics. First, Stickney did not know what either Senator Humphrey or Secretary Brannan would talk about at the meeting. Nor should it be overlooked that Senator Thye, a Republican opponent of the Brannan Plan, had been invited to address the convention.

Second, Stickney did arrange a morning session devoted to a discussion of the program then being administered by PMA.

Third, and most important, sound administrative planning involves more than mere didactic instruction; it also involves morale. Meetings addressed by the Secretary of Agriculture and other important agricultural figures (Senators Humphrey and Thye were both members of the Senate Agricultural Committee) doubtless make a valuable contribution to the *esprit de corps* of PMA committeemen. Whether or not this purpose was served by this particular meeting may be debatable, in view of the nature of the remarks by the principal speakers. Stickney, however, was not clairvoyant, and could not have foreseen the contents of the speeches.

That brings up Brannan's choice of this meeting as a vehicle for beating the drums on behalf of his Plan. It is difficult to rate this move as other than a lack of regard for the proprieties of responsible administration. A rip-roaring defense of the Brannan Plan may have whipped up enthusiasm for the Plan, but it could hardly have increased the ardor for a more effective administration of the existing law. And since many members must have been opposed to the Plan, it probably created resentment among some of them.

If it had been proper for Brannan to use this meeting for propaganda purposes, it would have been equally proper to have propagandized other state PMA meetings. This would have provided the Secretary a unique opportunity to reach influential farmers throughout the nation with his message. But it is extremely doubtful that such appearances would either promote more efficient administration or be consistent with the intention of Congress in appropriating the money for PMA state conventions.

Despite Brannan's publicly defensive attitude, there was general agreement in USDA and within PMA that the oratorical performances at the April 4 meeting had left the Department open to criticism. Senator Aiken's charges at least served the purpose of insuring more prudence in the conduct of future meetings.

CONCLUSIONS

What conclusions can fairly be drawn concerning the over-all publicity performance of USDA in relation to the Brannan Plan? Is it substantially true, as Representative Vorys said, that the Department had "all stops out to win national support for the Brannan Plan"?

Lacking adequate comparative data, it is not easy to generalize on the restraint or absence of restraint exercised by the Department in this area.[40] From the evidence presented, however, no such indictment as that made by Representative Vorys can be sustained.

The Secretary and his staff did make an impressive number

of speeches which were routinely reproduced as press releases and circulated quite widely among opinion-molders in the field of agriculture. USDA material on the Plan did directly reach many of the most influential farmers in the nation. But it is also true that the Department ordinarily and appropriately carries on a considerable information program for the benefit of agriculture, and with public attention centering upon the Brannan Plan, the latter would receive a substantial amount of publicity through the normal operation of USDA information channels.

Furthermore, USDA bureau organs carried a surprisingly small amount of informational material on the Plan. Credible evidence has yet to be furnished that PMA—with the possible exception of its activity in a few states—acted as an important propaganda medium for the Brannan Plan. Aside from Brannan's stepped-up speaking engagements, there appears to have been no extraordinary publicity effort by the Department to "sell" the Plan to the public.

IV

BRANNAN'S PLAN: DOWN
BUT NOT OUT

The Brannan Plan threw a scare into the Republican party. The Republicans had just suffered a humiliating defeat in the 1948 election and now it appeared that Brannan had come up with something that might appeal to both farmers and consumers. As one observer put it: "If the Democrats put this through, they'll be in for life."

The supposed political appeal of the Plan stemmed from a number of its facets. It offered to guarantee farmers—collectively—a high minimum income. The promise of lower prices on meat, eggs, and dairy products was expected to lure both labor and consumers. The guarantee of high price supports on corn, and of even higher supports on livestock, by means of which most corn is finally marketed, should please the corn belt. The shifting of farm program costs (in part) from a regressive tax on consumers to the graduated federal income tax brackets had potential popular appeal. Since small farmers greatly outnumber large ones, the apparent preferment given the former was regarded as a shrewd political stroke.

It was further believed by many agricultural observers that the proposal to junk flexible price supports fitted in with the farmers' current mood. Discerning politicians with an eye on the farm vote agreed that farm organizations looked with more favor upon flexible price supports than did the farmers themselves. The latter were seriously disturbed about declining prices, and the pocketbook pinch was beginning to have its characteristic effect on the farmers' aversion to "governmental-ism" in agriculture.

One significant political aspect of the Plan was quite generally overlooked. In dealing forthrightly with a vexing agricultural problem, Brannan had also produced a formula which might arrest or even reverse the growing rift between Southern and liberal elements within the Democratic party which had led to the "Dixiecrat" revolt in 1948. Specifically, the income support standard was translated into considerably higher price supports for tobacco than the 90 per cent of parity contained in Title I of the Agricultural Act of 1948, and much more generous supports than in Title II.[1] Slightly higher support levels than in Title I were also offered on cotton. Conceivably these proposals, in conjunction with features of the Plan pleasing to groups with liberal inclinations, could help hold together the coalition which had kept the Democratic party in power for twenty years. Failing this, it might at least provide a temporary alliance sufficiently strong to assure victory for the Brannan Plan.

For reasons to be explored later, the Farm Bureau could have been expected to furnish Brannan with powerful opposition. There was a time when the Bureau could stop in its tracks any farm legislation to which it was irreconcilably opposed. Although its strength had declined somewhat from its previous high-water mark, it was still a redoubtable adversary. Fortunately for Brannan, however, the Bureau had an Achilles' heel at which the Brannan Plan struck directly. Southern state Farm Bureau leaders dissented sharply from President Allan Kline's militant support of flexible price supports, although their minority status prevented their views from prevailing during the annual Farm Bureau conventions. The Brannan Plan's emphasis on fixed, high-level supports thus threatened to rupture the thin surface membrane of Farm Bureau unity by sharpening the internal conflict within that organization.

Furthermore, if Brannan's political instincts were sound, the Bureau would be conspicuously cast in a role of opposition to a "strong" farm price support program at a time when farmers were beginning to feel an urgent need for one. If this were to widen the split within the Bureau and undermine rank-and-file support for national Bureau leadership, neither Brannan nor the Southern Congressmen would lose any sleep over it.

The over-all strategy was bold, ingenious, and plausible. Blended of so many attractive and potent political ingredients, the Brannan Plan seemed assured of strong support from many diverse quarters. Yet not only was the total Plan rejected, but efforts to obtain a "trial run" for production payments failed to win Congressional support.

Many factors account for the political failure of the Plan. It would be impossible to place them, with any assurance of accuracy, in order of importance, and no attempt will be made to do so. However, the underlying reasons for the collapse of the Plan fall into the following main categories: the Farm Bureau, the National Grange, the powerful livestock interests, and certain key Congressional figures were predisposed to reject it; the income support level provided effective ammunition to Brannan's opponents; neither the farmer nor the general public really understood what the Plan was all about or how it would work; and economic developments did not proceed in accordance with Brannan's expectations.

The implacable opposition of the Farm Bureau to the Plan was virtually foreordained. The Bureau had no special love for Charles Brannan at the time of his appointment as Secretary of Agriculture. His principal field experience in the Department had been with the Farm Security Administration, an organization the Bureau had fought tooth and claw for years.[2] The Farm Security Administration served the interests of down-and-out farmers, whereas Bureau membership was composed of the more prosperous farmers. Although many small farmers were enrolled in the Bureau, the organizational leadership was drawn directly from the ranks of its more well-to-do members and partook of the psychology of "successful" American businessmen. One might say that the difference in philosophy between dedicated Farm Security Administration officials and Farm Bureau leaders was the difference between that of social workers and of Rotarians.

The Bureau was philosophical about Brannan's original appointment as Secretary, since it was confident that the Democratic administration was on the way out. It was much less complacent, however, when it faced the prospect of dealing with him for four long years. According to a number of sources, the Bureau was hoping to elevate its president, Allan Kline, to the secretaryship.[3] Or if not Kline, at least some one in the good graces of the Bureau. The galling aspects of the election were not mitigated by the selection of an all-star cast of Farmers Union officials for the President's inaugural farm committee.

The Bureau was acutely aware that Brannan was an old friend and favorite of James Patton, and that Patton had done everything in his power to obtain the post for Brannan. As president of the Farmers Union, Patton led an organization which feuded continuously with the Bureau. The bitterness between the two organizations found expression not only in efforts to discredit each other in the eyes of the farmers, but also in opposing positions on both agricultural and nonagricultural policies. The Farm Bureau sniped at the Farmers Union as a prolabor, left-wing (even Communistic) organization; and the latter retorted that the Bureau was the mouthpiece and tool of the biggest commercial farmers, and was harnessed with reactionary nonagricultural organizations.

That Brannan's close identification with the Farmers Union had not been altered by his appointment as Secretary of Agriculture soon became apparent to the Bureau. The parallels between the Brannan Plan and the positions recently taken by the Farmers Union were not lost upon it. There could be no doubt, if indeed there had ever been any, that both the President and the Secretary of Agriculture were married to the Bureau's bitterest enemy. This knowledge, combined with the paeans which the Farmers Union promptly began to sing on behalf of the Plan, served to snuff out any flickering sympathy which might have been entertained by Farm Bureau officialdom toward features of the Plan.

The leadership of the Farm Bureau, although officially neutral in politics, was unmistakably oriented toward the Republican party's conservative wing. Allan Kline's political and economic philosophy (as well as his crusading spirit) closely approximated that of former Senator Robert E. Taft, except that the Farm Bureau's president was more persuaded of the necessity for an internationalist trade policy.

As might be expected, Mr. Kline selected lieutenants who shared his intense suspicion of "Big Government." Nothing struck me more forcefully, in talking to high-ranking Farm Bureau officials in 1952, than the anti-governmentalist sentiments which colored their discussions of public policies.

In the pervasiveness of his conservatism, Kline differed somewhat from his predecessor, the redoubtable Ed O'Neal. The latter, described by Stuart Chase as the man who could "make more Congressmen run faster than any man alive," [4] did not permit his conservatism to stand in the way of his efforts to advance the immediate economic interests of the Farm Bureau. He was zealous in pursuing higher price supports, parity payments, and sundry governmental bounties for commercial farmers. On other legislative matters, however, his conservatism strongly asserted itself, clad in the typical clichés and stereotypes of many politicians arrayed on the American political Right.

Allan Kline's conservatism appeared to be of a more authentic type. It met the acid test by extending into areas affecting the immediate economic self-interest of the organization he represented. Under his leadership, the Bureau consistently fought to reduce appropriations for agriculture, and to keep price supports flexible and at moderate levels. It should be reiterated that this was done despite the fact, as Professor Hardin puts it, that "government agricultural policy in price support, in commodity loans, in marketing regulations, in research and extension, in soil conservation, and in governmental credit is largely designed and administered for the benefit of commercial farmers." [5] This rather remarkable example of a leading economic pressure group acting to restrain governmental assistance to its members is a phenomenon with few precedents in American history.

It would be erroneous to conclude that the Bureau's positions were divorced from power considerations. In many instances, the ideological preferences of the leadership inclined it to a course of action which also served its power interests. For example, the opposition to soil-conservation payments coincided with the Bureau's desire to weaken PMA, which administered these payments. The efforts to keep support levels at a point where acreage controls and marketing quotas are infrequently invoked served a similar purpose.

Bureau hostility to PMA can be traced to several factors. The Bureau was fearful that the PMA farmer committee system might be transformed into a rival farm organization.[6] Even if this development failed to materialize, PMA committees would wield administrative power which the Bureau could not readily control. The Bureau preferred to vest as much administrative power as possible in the Extension Service, with which it had close ties. Also of significance was PMA's decidedly Democratic tinge.[7]

It remains the belief of some observers, however, that the ideology of the leaders was a very real force in guiding the policies of the Bureau, and that this force acted to some extent independently of the power factors involved, and contrary to at least the short-run economic interests of organization members.

The Bureau had gone on record on several specific points virtually committing it to oppose the principles of the Brannan Plan. In 1945, with respect to support prices versus compensatory payments, it resolved: "We are unalterably opposed to plans which would propose unlimited production at ruinous prices and force the American farmers to depend permanently upon governmental subsidies." [8] Brannan did not propose "unlimited production at ruinous prices," nor did he intend that the farmer should be permanently dependent upon governmental subsidies. Nevertheless, the Farm Bureau position toward a combination of direct payments and a free market was seen to be antipathetic.

This attitude was also evident during the wartime dispute over the use of farm subsidies. Dr. Wilcox has pointed out:

"Throughout the war period the National Farmers Union has supported the use of subsidies in lieu of raising price ceilings to prevent increases in the cost of living. . . . In contrast, both the Farm Bureau and the National Grange insisted on the removal of subsidies in extensions of the Act." [9]

Bureau opposition to the direct payment–free market approach under Ed O'Neal partially reflected its antagonism, on political grounds, to any measure which would transfer the cost of agricultural benefits from the consumer to the taxpayer.[10] It also reflected the desire of farmers to preserve the feeling that their income was won by their own individual efforts.

Under Kline, hostility to direct payments was reinforced by the ideological desire to diminish direct financial relationships between government and farmer, relationships which might serve to erode the farmer's ingrained opposition to "bureaucrats" and governmentalism. But, perhaps of equal importance, the Bureau was not forgetful that production payments would be disbursed by officials of PMA. The Bureau could not view with equanimity any development which would tend to cultivate favorable farmer attitudes toward PMA and its county committees.

The Farm Bureau did not have a consistent record of opposition to direct government payments to agriculture. It had given express approval to the use of direct payments to supplement the income of sugar producers under the Sugar Act. And far from objecting to the parity payments under AAA, the Bureau had fought for them. The conditions differed materially, of course, from those proposed by Brannan. Having wrung the maximum price support advantage from Congress, the Bureau (under O'Neal) was happy to obtain whatever frosting direct payments could provide. In other words, direct payments as a supplement to price supports were all right; as a substitute, they were unacceptable.

Similarly, the Bureau (again under O'Neal) had favored generous soil-conservation payments. Nor had it raised any objections to the inclusion of the following phraseology in the Aiken Act: "The Secretary, through the Commodity Credit Corporation . . . is authorized to support prices of agricultural com-modities to producers through loans, purchases, *payments,* and other operations." (Italics mine.) Allan Kline, it should be noted, was at the Bureau's helm in 1948. And Mr. Kline, ac-cording to Loren Soth's excellent volume, *Farm Trouble,* once "expressed mild approval of the idea [direct payments combined with a free market], at least as worth trying out."

There has been a great deal of dispute concerning Congres-sional intentions in inserting the word "payments" in the 1948 Act.[11] Discussing the Brannan Plan on the floor of the Senate, Senator Aiken made the following clarifying statement: "The recommendation for making payments to farmers as an alterna-tive for purchasing or loaning on the crop is already contained in the 1948 act. This method of supporting prices, if used care-fully, will permit consumers to benefit from bountiful crops and low prices without unduly penalizing the producer or the taxpayer." [12]

The Senator's comment was made, significantly, on April 7, 1949, before passions were aroused which led to hindsight inter-pretations of a questionable nature. To clinch the point, Sena-tor Aiken outlined "four radical departures from the provisions of the Agricultural Act of 1948," without including Brannan's proposal for production payments among them.[13]

Under these circumstances, the violence of the Bureau's re-action to this facet of the Brannan Plan invites a measure of suspicion. It is possible, however, that the Bureau expected such payments as were made under the Aiken Act to be used only in unusual circumstances—not to become the standard method by which producers of 50 per cent of the value of farm produce were to have their income permanently protected.

Brannan had proposed to continue price supports for major storable commodities, reserving direct payments for selected perishables. In view of the difficulties of adapting price supports to perishables, the Bureau, under other circumstances, might have taken a more sympathetic attitude toward the limited use of production payments. But Brannan, in his early committee testimony, had indicated that "it might be advisable on occasion to have the production payment available for use for storable commodities." [14] Later, in a symposium conducted by the National Farm Institute in Des Moines, Iowa, Brannan asserted that he "would like to use production payments on cotton immediately." [15] Although the use of direct payments for storable commodities was not the central core of Brannan's thinking, these remarks gave the Bureau an excuse for charging that Brannan ultimately proposed to substitute production payments for price supports on all commodities. This simplified Bureau strategy, and enabled it to lash out in an unqualified attack upon the Brannan Plan.

The Bureau had given vigorous support to the moderate and flexible support levels in the Aiken Act. After the 1948 election, and before the emergence of the Brannan Plan, it reaffirmed its support of the act and its opposition to fixed, high-level price supports.[16] At an earlier period, however, under Ed O'Neal, it had taken a somewhat different position. In 1939, the foreword to the resolutions of the Farm Bureau declared: "We believe that failure to raise agriculture's income to parity is the major cause of the unemployment which has cost the Federal Government billions of dollars in relief appropriations.

"The unsettled conditions of the world makes it increasingly imperative that the United States should put its domestic affairs in order without further delay. The cost of accomplishing this by restoring agriculture to complete parity is hardly a drop in the bucket compared to the cost of neglecting to do the one thing which will solve our difficulties." [17]

Any reasonable interpretation of this position would align it more closely to Brannan's income support standard, and the rationale supporting it, than to the Bureau position in 1949. The Bureau stand in 1949, however, faithfully represented Allan Kline's conviction that it is not the government's responsibility to guarantee profitable prices to any economic group, and that any attempt to do so only invites disaster in the long run. Opposition by Bureau leadership to the Secretary's income support level sprang out of well-rooted conviction, therefore, and not merely out of animosity toward Brannan himself.

Judging from its general economic philosophy and orientation, the Bureau could have been depended on to cast a jaundiced eye on the 1800-unit rule. This likelihood was not lessened by the fact that Kline, in his capacity as a farmer, would have personally felt the bite of its application.[18] The conditioning of price and income support benefits upon maintenance of minimum soil-conservation practices was likewise unsatisfactory to the Bureau. Since the county PMA committees would administer this provision, its enactment would result in driving PMA roots deeper into the agricultural program and into farm communities.

The manner in which the Brannan Plan was formulated put the finishing touches on the Bureau's antipathy to it. The latter castigated "the unusual procedure employed in creating this plan" [19]—that feature being the Plan's delivery without the benefit of Farm Bureau midwifery.[20] USDA failure to consult the major farm organizations in the origination of policy proposals was in itself an inexcusable practice, in the Bureau's opinion. And when partisan administration officials came forth with independently conceived policy proposals in the field of agriculture, this had "the effect of throwing the farm problem into the partisan political arena, a situation which we deplore and condemn." [21]

Brannan's answer was concisely stated in a letter to Joseph and Stewart Alsop, who had criticized his failure to consult with the farm organizations: "Congress wanted the opinions of the Secretary of Agriculture and of no one else at that time. They already had their own opinions and I assume that they were as familiar with the farm leaders' opinions as I was. But they did not ask me to pull together the widely differing views of farm economists, organizations and Congressmen. As a matter of fact, that is the function of Congress." [22]

The Bureau's attitude toward the "unusual procedure employed in creating this Plan" was in part a reaction to the implications which it saw in the Brannan Plan that the Bureau was not properly representing the desires and interests of American farmers. That "bureaucrats" should presume to tell

Congress that farmers wanted, or needed, a farm program drastically differing from that espoused by the Bureau struck the latter as a reflection upon its own representative character and wisdom. Had Brannan's proposals received little publicity, the Bureau could have shrugged them off, or even quietly absorbed acceptable portions into its own program. But since the Plan became front-page news and picked up impressive national support, it was necessary to demonstrate that Brannan was wrong—wrong in reading the farmers' mind and wrong in presuming that his judgment was superior to that of the Bureau.

No organization as powerful as the Farm Bureau could look with anything but the gravest apprehension upon major farm-policy shifts in which it had not played a significant role. The Bureau exists primarily to serve the legislative interests of its members. Any public demonstration that it was failing to do this, or that legislative policy was moving out of the orbit of its influence and control, would have serious repercussions upon its institutional status. If substantial changes were made in agricultural policy, changes to which the Bureau could not give at least the color of collaboration, it would inevitably lose standing among its members and with the farming community in general. This fact accounts for much of the animosity the Bureau felt toward Charles Brannan and the Brannan Plan. It also helps to explain why previous secretaries had tended to funnel their policy recommendations *through* the farm organizations to Congress, instead of carrying them directly to Congress.

Another closely allied factor must be considered in rounding out the picture. The Bureau's grievance was not only that Brannan had offered independently conceived recommendations on agricultural policy, but that he had then proceeded to fight for them, in conjunction with allies which raised the Bureau's hackles on sight. Four days after the unveiling of the Brannan Plan, J. Howard McGrath, chairman of the Democratic National Committee, made a ringing endorsement of the Plan.[23] From that point on, the Brannan proposals were clearly labeled "Democratic," with all the advantages and liabilities pertaining thereto. Although the Democratic party did not formally endorse the Plan, President Truman gave it strong support, the Women's Division of the National Committee carried on a very intensive campaign on its behalf, and the party organized two regional conferences in which the Plan was given priority and favorable consideration.

One of the more constant factors in American social experience has been agriculture's spirit of enmity toward labor unions. This spirit had been accentuated by the emergence of the outspokenly liberal CIO Political Action Committee as a major political force. The conspicuous participation of this organization at the Des Moines meeting, in conjunction with the Bureau's arch-enemy, the Farmers Union, provided a setting which destined the Bureau to blow fire from both nostrils. It would have been hard enough for the Bureau to adopt a temperate attitude toward any major farm-policy revisions which Brannan might propose, and impossible for it to curb its instincts when Brannan was teamed up with the Democratic party, the Farmers Union, and the CIO Political Action Committee!

The Des Moines meeting heightened the impression, already current, that Brannan's proposals were receiving their most enthusiastic reception from the Fair Deal wing of the Party. This meeting hastened the congealing of forces within and without agriculture which are inherently allergic to any program with strong liberal and labor support.

The feud between Brannan and the Bureau reached towering proportions. There is no need to recite the long list of explosive verbal exchanges which marked this rather remarkable battle between the most powerful governmental figure and the most powerful organizational unit in agriculture. To illustrate the intensity of the emotions involved, however, the following is quoted from a speech made by the Secretary before the National Farm Institute at Des Moines, Iowa, on February 18, 1950:

Because the gentleman now heading the American Farm Bureau is here today, I would like to take the opportunity, for just this once, of addressing him directly in the hope of reaching a better understanding of the attitude of the Farm Bureau's present national leadership.

I would like to ask the President of the American Farm Bureau Federation, in all seriousness: Does it aid agriculture in any way to say of the Administration's proposals: "People who propose such a program to farmers are very dumb or downright dishonest"?

How will such personal attacks protect the price of hogs?

I would like to ask the gentleman: Do you actually expect to halt the decline in farm prices by calling the Administration's recommendations a "statement of politico-economic philosophy—not a farm program," a "supreme delusion," or, as you have also done by saying the idea is "nuts"?

I would like to ask the gentleman: Do you think it fair to your own members to be openly favoring still lower price supports for farmers in the harsh hope of forcing some of them out of business, so that farming can be more profitable for those big-scale farmers with larger cash reserves who are able to survive?

I would also like to ask: Do you feel the Farm Bureau is fulfilling a constructive role in behalf of agriculture by having its spokesmen spend their time tearing down the recommendations of others with such abusive remarks as, and again I quote, "It shines and stinks and stinks and shines like the rotten mackerel in the moonlight"? . . .

I might venture to suggest that instead of sitting in the seat of the scornful, adopting a tone of antagonism or condescension, or assuming a cocksure attitude that carries its own condemnation, the gentleman might better serve agriculture by recognizing earnest efforts for a better farm program in the making; and that in a constructive spirit he should make contributions toward wise development of its policy.[24]

While the resources of the National Grange were not mustered against the Brannan Plan with either the thoroughness or the political effectiveness of the Farm Bureau, Grange opposition was nevertheless of some importance. The political philosophy of Grange spokesmen closely paralleled that of the Farm Bureau at that time. The Grange, moreover, appears to have originated the flexible price support formula,[25] and it did not propose to abandon this principle in the face of attacks upon it by liberal elements in the Democratic party.[26] Furthermore, during the Congressional hearings on long-range agricultural policy, the Grange had registered its disapproval of agricultural benefits via direct payments.

Brannan was not the victim of any illusions about the reception his proposals would receive from livestock interests. The latter had never asked Congress for price or income protection, and they were proud of the fact. In considerable measure, of course, their willingness to accept the risks of the free market had been enhanced by the fact that the odds had been in their favor for many years. Gambling is no doubt most pleasant when the prospects are narrowed down to "Will I make a good profit, or will it be a killing?"

The cattlemen's aversion to the federal government had deep roots. For many years they had been engaged in a heated battle with the Forest Service over the management and use of federally owned grazing lands. The Forest Service was interested in conservation; the cattlemen, in profits. Friction was therefore inevitable and more or less continuous. During the war, moreover, the government employed direct subsidies to keep meat prices down while maintaining industry profits at a sufficient level to encourage maximum output. The cattle raisers strenuously opposed this practice, characteristically preferring to let prices rise to their natural levels. Although they resented subsidies, most of their wrath centered upon the hapless Office of Price Administration, which they regarded as a bureaucratic conspiracy against their rightful interests.

Quite naturally, then, the livestock industry leaders fought the Brannan Plan vigorously and from the start. Their opposition to federal income protection in any form hurt the Plan's chances, since Congress is of course reluctant to thrust protection on a group which doesn't want it.

The argument over the income support standard was soon narrowed down to the relative merits of fixed price supports and flexible price supports.[27] This was not the battleground upon which Brannan's enemies preferred to joust. There was too much evidence that farmers were genuinely uneasy about flexible supports, especially in a period of falling prices. The South had shown its distaste for flexible supports in the legislative session of 1948, and powerful Republicans in the House of Representatives, led by Representative Hope, had joined the South in this controversy. If Brannan's opponents were to concentrate their fire on high-level price and income supports, forces potentially hostile to the Plan could not be rallied together.

The most pressing agricultural problem at the time was how to handle the accumulating purchases of perishables. This problem was magnified by the possibility that hog purchases would soon become necessary under existing legislative commitments. Congress, therefore, chose to wrestle first with production payments, leaving other aspects of the Brannan Plan to await a future decision. Since much of the political attractiveness of the Plan centered around income protection and a free market for perishable producers, and since pending administrative difficulties were becoming acute, Brannan was willing to meet the enemy on this political terrain. This also coincided with the wishes of the anti-Brannan forces, for it enabled them to discharge their strongest propaganda artillery and marshal their most potent political combination against the Plan.[28]

There were a number of reasons for this. Potential opponents were unhampered by any prior commitments to the principle of production payments and a free market. The politically damaging charges concerning "regimentation," exorbitant costs, and government "handouts" could conveniently focus on production payments. Finally, farmers themselves were believed to be in a state of latent hostility to direct payments. There was less probability, therefore, of Brannan and his supporters setting a successful backfire in the grass roots.

Gradually, with Brannan's co-operation, the controversy over the Brannan Plan tended to center on production payments. Before the smoke of battle had cleared away, the terms "production payments" and "Brannan Plan" had become almost synonymous in the public mind. And as production payments came to the fore, the level of support tended more and more to recede into the background, or to be blended into the continuing argument over fixed versus flexible price supports.

With the battle lines so drawn, the struggle over production payments became crucial to both sides. If provision for their use were legislatively ratified, Brannan would be popularly regarded as having won a great victory. If they were rejected, Brannan and his supporters would be repudiated. This gave inadequate recognition to Brannan's considerable range of objectives, but it was the natural outcome of the power struggle which the Brannan Plan had precipitated.

Had the Brannan Plan not become a partisan issue, Brannan might have won at least a partial victory. Since the main impact of the Plan upon the South was to raise and stabilize the support level of tobacco and cotton, while leaving the method of support unchanged, the Plan met instant favor with Representative Harold D. Cooley of North Carolina, chairman of the House of Agriculture Committee, and with Representative Stephen Pace of Georgia, chairman of the subcommittee directed to hold hearings on the Plan. Although Representative Cooley made it clear that the 1800-unit rule would never be approved by Congress, he paid glowing tribute to Brannan's testimony.[29]

Representative Hope was also favorably inclined toward many features of the Plan, as was indicated by his comments during the earlier hearings on the Brannan Plan. He agreed with Brannan's rejection of flexible supports. And as the leading Republican exponent of high-level price supports, he declared: "As long as support prices do not exceed parity, nonfarmers and consumers cannot complain." Brannan's income support standard, it will be recalled, would have averaged slightly below 100 per cent of modernized parity during the first years it was to have been effective. Hope had also expressed the view that the government's obligation to protect the producers of perishable commodities was just as great as it was to protect the producers of the basic commodities. While he had indicated no approval of production payments, nothing in his earlier committee statements indicated that he was opposed to them if circumstances made them the only feasible alternative to vast government purchase programs.

In discussing the 1800-unit rule, Hope seemed to be in general agreement with the principle of limiting income support to a given amount of production. At one point, in fact, he appeared to approve a suggestion that the law pertaining to acreage allotments be amended to limit production to an amount not exceeding the 1800-unit limit.[30]

In brief, Representative Hope, the most influential House Republican on agricultural questions, was inclined to be sympathetic with the most important parts of the Brannan proposals. His principal objection to the Plan, judging by his earlier remarks in committee, was not based on its substantive features, but on semantics. He was fearful that abandoning the parity symbol would imperil popular support for the farm program.

Senator Anderson was predisposed to take a critical view of the Brannan Plan. He had supported the principles of the Aiken Act, and regarded them as generally consistent with the best judgment of the Department of Agriculture. His unhappy experience, while Secretary of Agriculture, with managing the price support program for potatoes at inflexible levels, deepened his conviction that rigid price supports were unwise and dangerous. He had specifically warned the Congress against placing supports too high, and had suggested that 75 per cent of parity might be about right. Earlier, too, he had aligned himself in opposition to direct payments as a substitute for price supports.

Anderson also recognized, or thought he recognized, the guiding hand of James Patton in the Brannan Plan. That there was bad blood between Anderson and Patton [31] was common knowledge around Washington, and this fact was bound to influence Anderson's attitude toward the Plan. Finally, a former cabinet officer is not likely to be gratified by proposals put forward by his immediate successor recommending drastic policy changes.

Although Senator Elmer Thomas (D–Okla.), chairman of the Senate Committee on Agriculture and Forestry, promptly lined up behind the Plan, he did not wield as much power with either the Committee or with Senate Democrats as did Senator Anderson. The latter had had a successful tour of duty as Secretary of Agriculture, enjoyed a reputation as a sound man, and his voice carried great weight in the agricultural councils of the Democratic party.

Anderson followed a very restrained course in connection with the Brannan Plan. After tipping his hand during the opening hearings, he was privately requested by President Truman to hold his fire, at least until Brannan had had a chance to present his views more fully.[32] Anderson thereupon issued a curious statement which read in part as follows:

> On second reading of Secretary Brannan's recommendations I am struck by the fact that they grow in attractiveness and interest as they are studied.
>
>   .   .   .   .   .
>
> I have not endorsed Secretary Brannan's program as yet because I want to study it thoroughly and to see that the Congress has the opportunity to study it also. . . . I believe his suggestions will grow in favor as they become more thoroughly understood.[33]

For a considerable period thereafter, he refused to take a generalized position for or against the Plan, although Senate cloakroom gossip had it that Anderson would not give the Plan his support.

Senator Aiken, ranking Republican member of the Senate Committee on Agriculture and Forestry, father of the Agricultural Act of 1948, and a staunch believer in flexible price supports, was not expected to endorse the Plan. His initial reaction, however, indicates that he was somewhat impressed with Brannan's handiwork. Apparently anticipating that it would have great popular appeal, he delivered a speech in the Senate emphasizing the many parallels between it and his own Act.[34]

Reference has already been made to Senator Aiken's statement that the Brannan Plan bore close resemblance to Title II of the Agricultural Act of 1948, which Aiken himself had sponsored. He expressed satisfaction with the use of production payments and observed that his Act, as well as Brannan's proposals, gave impetus to the expansion of livestock agriculture as a means of utilizing grain surpluses and raising dietary levels. The principle of limiting support to a given amount of production had "merit," in his opinion, and he held that the decision to move price supports from a parity base to an income base was in line with instructions specifically contained in existing law. Furthermore, he insisted that the 1948 Act called upon the Secretary of Agriculture to support meat and dairy products on a level of equality with basic commodities.[35] Although he did not endorse fixed, high-level price supports, he frequently referred to the fact that the so-called "sliding scale" in the 1948 Act could be disregarded at the discretion of the Secretary of Agriculture.

While Senator Aiken registered strong opposition to the level of Brannan's support standard, disapproved of the soil-conservation requirement, and doubted the workability of the 1800-unit rule, his attitude toward the Plan was not, originally, one of implacable hostility. Had the element of partisanship not entered the picture, he might have found it possible to support a compromise between his Act and the Brannan Plan. Certainly it would have been easy for him to approve production payments as representing the flowering of a principle he was already on record as favoring in appropriate instances.

Aiken, however, became convinced that Brannan was playing politics, and this aroused his combative instincts. He felt that the Secretary could have carried out most of his program within the framework of the Aiken Act, and that his refusal to do so was evidence of a purely partisan desire to get the Aiken Act off the books. Accordingly, in the heat of the battle which developed, Aiken began to soft-pedal the similarities between his Act and the Brannan Plan, and to excoriate the latter as a thoroughly unsound approach. "The Republican party," he stated on August 24, 1950, in an obvious slap at the Plan, "has always opposed measures designed to force the farmer to a state of abject dependency upon government or which would put him under strict totalitarian controls." [36]

Representative Hope, also a staunch and loyal Republican, joined in the attacks on production payments after the Brannan Plan became a partisan issue. Conveniently, he overlooked the fact that the evils which he attributed to production payments should have been charged to the account of the support level accompanying them—a level to which he could not, with any show of consistency, object!

If Southern agricultural spokesmen—or moderate elements within the Democratic party—had been persuaded to man the forefront of the political battle, prospects for passage of Brannan's program would have brightened considerably. As it was, the conspicuous and vigorous backing of liberal organizations such as the CIO Political Action Committee appears to have helped accomplish what Brannan's foes sought above all else— a split in Southern Democratic ranks. Whether or not the propaganda campaign was consciously designed with this in mind, the political Right's relentless hammering away at "CIO dictation of agricultural policy" and at "socialistic left-wing agricultural planners," made potentially pro-Brannan Southern Congressmen uneasy.

Politics makes strange bedfellows, but sharing the bed with inveterate foes is tolerable only when there are no acceptable alternatives. Happily for wriggling Southerners, a bill sponsored by Representative Albert S. Gore (D–Tenn.) provided a convenient escape from the taint of popular identification with Brannan's "left-wing" supporters. Since this bill called for a continuation of the fixed, high-level supports in which the South was mainly interested—and did not bear the stigma believed to be attached to the Brannan Plan—Southern representatives not already committed to Brannan's proposals rallied behind it. Uncertainty about the program for perishables tempered their satisfaction with the Gore Bill, but support of the latter seemed preferable for the present to being numbered with those from the political pest-house. Besides, an increasing number of Congressmen were of the opinion that public sentiment was crystallizing against the Plan.

Backers of the Brannan Plan united behind the so-called Brannan-Pace Bill reported out by the House Committee on Agriculture. This bill would have given Brannan's proposals, minus the 1800-unit rule and the soil-conservation requirement, a "trial run" on potatoes, wool, and eggs. Earlier efforts to include hogs in the "trial run" had collapsed, largely because of concern about the possible repercussion of low hog prices on the prices of other meat products.

Although the Farm Bureau remained officially adamant in its opposition to fixed, high-level, price supports, it now proceeded to give powerful behind-the-scenes encouragement for the Gore Bill in an effort to block the Brannan-Pace measure. The Bureau was grimly determined to deny Brannan the fruits of even partial victory; if support of the Gore Bill was the means to that end, that bill must be embraced. The Bureau was gambling heavily, too, that the support system for perishables would manage to survive the stresses of the coming year.

Representative Cooley, chairman of the House Committee on Agriculture, had stated during the course of the debate on the Brannan-Pace Bill: "In the fifteen years that I have been on this committee not one single solitary time have we met defeat at the hands of the House of Representatives." [37] Now, although leading Democratic members of the Committee gave strong support to the bill, and Speaker Sam Rayburn took the floor in one of his infrequent appearances to announce: "I found out a long time ago that in this House the people get along the best who go along the most," the Committee was headed for defeat. Republicans opposed the "trial run" idea almost to a man, spurred by a notice from the minority whip which read: "Every Republican member who is on his feet and breathing, or shows any signs of life and is free from doctor's orders must be accounted for on the above-mentioned dates, and be ready to vote on this important and far-reaching legislation. We must defeat the Brannan farm bill. It can be done if all Republicans are on the job." [38]

Content with the knowledge that the Brannan Plan had strengthened their hand in the struggle for fixed, high-level, price supports, enough Southern Democrats were constrained to join Republican members to insure scotching the Brannan-Pace Bill. The final vote was 239–170.

In view of the impressive alliance which had been built up against the Plan—the Republican party, many Democrats, the NAM and U.S. Chamber of Commerce, the American Farm

Bureau Federation, the National Grange, the National Co-operative Milk Producers Federation, the National Council of Farmer Cooperatives, and numerous livestock and commodity organizations, the conservative "educational" foundations, most of the rural press, and the overwhelming majority of newspapers and periodicals—the only hope for eventual passage of the Plan lay in the possibility of a grass-roots ground swell. But the latter failed to materialize. On July 30, 1949, Dr. George Gallup, Director of the American Institute of Public Opinion, reported, "Midwest farmers who have followed the discussion about the controversial Brannan farm subsidy plan are evenly divided in their opinions about it." On February 15, 1950, Dr. Gallup announced that of 27 per cent of the voters who "followed any of the discussions about the Brannan farm-price support," 8 per cent approved, 15 per cent disapproved, and 4 per cent had no opinion. [39]

An extensive speaking tour undertaken by Secretary Brannan, on President Truman's suggestion, combined with the continued slippage of farm prices, may have had some effect on farmers' views, however. The *New York Times* reported on May 14, 1950: "There are some clues . . . that farmer sentiment has shifted in the last year, although the margin in favor of the Brannan program is small. The clues are seen, not only in polls taken in Iowa, Wisconsin and elsewhere by farm publications, but in hard-bitten farmer statements, in milder statements of farm leaders and in a reshuffling of attitudes in key rural areas close to urban centers." [40] Whether or not this trend would have reached dimensions forcing more favorable Congressional considerations of Brannan's proposals, no one can say. At any rate, the Korean conflict, which rapidly melted away government surpluses of eggs and butter, and led to an immediate strengthening of farm prices, dealt the death blow to any lingering hopes that the Brannan Plan would be enacted during Brannan's tenure as Secretary of Agriculture.

Why did farmers fail to respond to the supposed political appeal of the Brannan Plan? As usual, a complex of factors was involved. The almost solid phalanx of farm organization opposition played an indeterminable, though no doubt significant, part. Organized labor's support of the Plan enabled Brannan's opponents to exploit latent suspicions among farmers. Third—and this may have been of prime importance—farmers were confused by the Plan. Only a tiny percentage of them understood the income support standard and its relationship to their familiar and beloved symbol, parity. One study showed that only 14 per cent of the farmers even knew that direct payments were involved in the Plan! [41] Farmers were also dubious about a Plan which appeared to offer both cheaper food and higher farm income, fearing that it must contain something sinister which did not meet the eye.

The "consumer subsidy" misconception appears to have contributed materially to the discrediting of the Brannan Plan. The Scripps-Howard papers, for example, carried an effective cartoon showing a Brannan cow with two udders, one for the farmer and one for the consumer. Unremitting attacks upon the "fallacy" this supposedly represented led many to believe that Brannan was indulging in cheap political legerdemain, and that his Plan was an example of "moral bankruptcy."

Actually, Brannan was on much firmer ground than his critics in this aspect of the controversy, but he never succeeded in putting his point across. To some extent, his job was complicated by the fact that the Democratic National Committee and some others were making exaggerated claims concerning the consumer benefits flowing from the Plan. Brannan himself never promised cheap food. He said only that the consumer would fare better under his proposal than under price support. In this he was undoubtedly right, again assuming equivalent income protection under a system of price supports.

The high level of the income support standard played a significant part in the defeat of the Plan. By setting his sights too high, Brannan lost potential support from many who were outside the orbit of the power struggle involved. These persons and groups might have tipped the balance of power to Brannan had

a more moderate income goal been established. As it was, Brannan found himself cut off from most nonliberal sources of support—and from many influential liberals as well.

In several instances, Brannan challenged those who attacked
his income support standard to suggest a more acceptable one
which would still serve the nation's interests. Although he made
this gesture, he also stated: "I am almost ashamed to confess that
the program I have proposed would let farm prices go down in
relation to other prices to such an extent that farm products
would have 15 per cent less purchasing power than they had
last year."

While the Brannan Plan suffered a crushing defeat in Congress, this can not be construed as a total failure on Brannan's
part to achieve any of his objectives. There is no way of determining the influence Brannan's income support standard, or his
attacks upon the sliding scale, had upon the nation and upon
Congress. There can be no reasonable doubt, however, that his
role stiffened the opposition to flexible price supports. The ele-
vation of minimum price support levels for basic commodities
from 60 per cent of parity in Title II of the Agricultural Act of
1948 to 75 per cent of parity in the Agricultural Act of 1949,
as well as the continued postponement of the date on which
flexible supports were to become effective, are probably partly
attributable to Brannan's efforts.

Some persons were inclined to credit Brannan with the
strengthening of price supports for milk and butter in the Agricultural Act of 1949. Whereas milk and butter enjoyed discretionary price support within a range of zero per cent to 90 per
cent of parity under Title II of the Agricultural Act of 1948,
mandatory support between 75 per cent and 90 per cent of
parity was provided in the Agricultural Act of 1949. Again, the
Brannan Plan may have been primarily responsible—or this
development may have been impending anyway. It seems reasonable to believe that the Secretary gave momentum to a trend
already underway.

The promises of both presidential candidates in the 1952
elections to search for a way to give equality of protection to

producers of perishable commodities is evidence that the Brannan Plan controversy sharpened interest in and demand for this goal. But the bitter campaign attacks upon the Plan by Dwight D. Eisenhower in 1952 [42] and the unwillingness of Adlai Stevenson to speak a good word for it in either the 1952 or 1956 campaigns are indirect, but reliable, indications of the disrepute into which the idea of production payments had fallen as a result of the furor over the Brannan Plan. The direct payment–free market principle had become charged with so much prejudice that Brannan's efforts may have actually delayed the establishment of an effective income support system for producers of perishable products.

Despite the political obstacles confronted by any farm legislation smacking of the Brannan Plan, Brannan received a measure of vindication in 1954 when Congress, with the approval of Secretary of Agriculture Ezra Taft Benson and most Republicans, authorized a system of compensatory payments for the income support of wool growers. (The *Wall Street Journal* called this system "The Brannan Plan in sheep's clothing.")

In recent years, moreover, Brannan-like proposals keep cropping up in Congress and elsewhere with a persistence that pays tribute to the hardihood of Brannan's Plan. Hog growers, disturbed by the booms and busts of their business, but dubious of the utility of price supports, cast increasingly longing glances at income stabilization via direct payments. Organizations representing the cotton industry gave strong support in 1957 to a bill which would have substituted direct payments for price supports, hoping to put cotton on a stronger competitive footing in both the world and the domestic market. But for the opposition of Secretary Benson, the bill stood a good chance of becoming law.

The dairy provisions of the House Committee on Agriculture's omnibus bill of 1958 also contained provisions calling for direct payments to dairy farmers, although by quite a different method than that proposed by Brannan.

As this book goes to press, prospects for the eventual adoption of a modified Brannan Plan appear brighter than ever. There can be no doubt that American agriculture is currently approaching a major policy crisis. The Benson program of reducing government controls and lowering price supports has led to a farm surplus stockpile valued at $9 billion (and still rising), a USDA budget of $7 billion (including over $1 billion for storage and handling costs alone), and declining farm income. It has also led many students of agriculture to question Benson's thesis that surpluses are primarily the product of the price support system, and that a virtually free market, combined with USDA salesmanship abroad, will create the conditions and markets which are the farmers' true salvation.

In the first place, it is becoming more and more apparent that it is the scientist rather than the system of price supports which is primarily to blame for farm surpluses. Recent advances in American production technology have been more spectacular in agriculture than in almost any other phase of American industry. Improved machinery, insecticides, fertilizers, seeds, chemical weed killers, the use of antibiotics in livestock feed, the spread of artificial insemination and other improved breeding practices—these and other technological developments primarily account for the amazing productivity of American agriculture. Technology largely explains why crop production in 1958, although it involved the fewest acres in 40 years, exceeded previous records by about 11 per cent. Technology also principally accounts for the fact that annual farm output is increasing considerably faster than increases in demand, despite the high birth rate and the inroads which highway and housing programs are making into our supply of arable land.

As for the comfortable assumption that lower price supports will induce the backward, marginal farmer to seek greener pastures in the city, leaving the more competent farmers to bask on a plateau of comparative prosperity, some reputable studies show that it is the presence of off-the-farm job opportunities, rather than low farm prices, which accelerates the exodus from the farm. For that matter, whenever less efficient farmers decide to call it quits, their land is usually purchased by the more efficient, whose enlarged holdings and superior farming practices enable them to get more production out of the newly acquired land than it formerly yielded. This does not reduce surpluses.

Benson's theory, it is conceded, might work if it were carried to its logical conclusion. Dr. Walter W. Wilcox of the Legislative Reference Service, Library of Congress, and one of the nation's foremost students of agriculture, has calculated that a completely free market would slash net farm income by from 25 to 40 per cent.[43] This in turn might cut farm production by 1) touching off a wave of bankruptcies and farm foreclosures, and 2) putting most remaining farmers in such straitened economic circumstances that they could not obtain the credit they need, or buy new machinery, or otherwise take advantage of the latest technological discoveries. No doubt there is a point at which agriculture becomes so financially depressed that output will fall. But is this really the way to solve the problem?

Now that a major policy overhaul has become both a political and economic imperative, Congress would be guilty of gross negligence if it failed to explore fully the promising potentialities of the free market–direct payment principle. According to persistent reports, Congress will not allow the indictment to be drawn.

A full-dress agricultural policy reappraisal is scheduled for 1960, and some competent observers believe Senators Humphrey of Minnesota and Talmadge of Georgia will unite a large segment of both the Northern and Southern wings of the Democratic party behind a free market–direct payment plan. Vigorous behind-the-scenes efforts, encouraged by Senate Majority Leader Lyndon Johnson, have been going forward this year to bring about such a development. Columnist Joseph Alsop has even been bold enough to prophesy that a modified Brannan Plan is almost a certainty to find its way into the Democratic party's national platform in 1960.

There are a variety of methods by which the free market–direct payment principle might be applied. It could be used for certain commodities in conjunction with an expanded soil conservation reserve, with a payment ceiling of, say, $12,000 to keep costs in line and individual subsidies at defensible levels. (Such a ceiling would protect farmers' *net* income up to only about $4,000 to $5,000.) Or payments could be limited to that portion of the output which is domestically consumed, as Senator Herman Talmadge of Georgia has proposed (again with an appropriate ceiling on payments). Economist George E. Brandow has suggested that marketing allotments might be established for producers of certain commodities, with payments based on perhaps 90 per cent of modernized parity for about 75 per cent of the marketing quota.[44] (If combined with a proper payments ceiling, fears that this would lead to unduly accelerated production and excessive costs might well prove groundless.)

A compensatory payment plan applied to livestock producers alone might yield surprisingly favorable results. If our staggering grain supplies were moved into the market in a properly regulated flow this would lead to a major increase in livestock production and a major drop in livestock prices. Payments to livestock producers could sustain livestock farmer incomes at satisfactory levels at the same time that consumers were enjoying substantially cheaper meat. Eventually the high level of livestock production might catch up with feed supplies and lead to feed grain prices at reasonably profitable levels without price supports. Meanwhile, Southern farmers would be encouraged to enlarge their livestock operations, thus reducing the urge to overproduce cotton, and diminishing the necessity for a cotton acreage control program.

The possible advantages to the consumer, the farmer, and the harassed USDA under some variation of the Brannan Plan formula are simply too great for the nation to ignore any longer. Compared to the inexcusable distress which the free market would bring, and the endless complications, contradictions and over-all costs of the price support system, a modified Brannan Plan would fairly reek of common sense. As University of Minnesota agricultural economist Willard Cochrane has put it, "This is the rational approach to income protection for agriculture."[45]

V

OBSERVATIONS

The travails endured by the Brannan Plan point up a number of important questions for observers of American political institutions and processes. What part should USDA have in the planning of public policy? What should be the Department's relation to private farm organizations during the policy-formulating process? To what extent, if any, should USDA act as a pressure influence on behalf of the clientele it serves?

There are a number of reasons for defending the right and asserting the responsibility of any federal department to participate actively in policy formulations affecting its sphere of interest. It can be demonstrated, moreover, that initiative in formulating comprehensive program recommendations and in presenting them to the Congress requires this activity.

Administrators who breathe the breath of life into legislative statutes have insights denied those who are less intimately associated with a given program. It would be as unwise to disregard these insights as it would be to overlook the protective and expansive characteristics which too often are exhibited by the custodians of governmental as well as of private institutions.[1]

Those who administer a public policy know from firsthand (and often painful) experience the administrative problems which must be solved if the purposes sought by Congress are to be fulfilled. They are in a position to know how effectively or ineffectively the expressed will of Congress is being achieved in practice.

But beyond this, conscientious, imaginative administrators become aware of related problems which are not being met, and of related opportunities for valuable public service. They may come to see that only peripheral problems are being dealt with, or that symptoms are being treated instead of diseases. Having these perceptions, it is only natural that they would begin to think in terms of a modified legislative program. And in casting about for answers to problems, they are bound to come up with suggestions worthy of public consideration.[2]

If this be true—and it seems beyond challenge—should administrators be denied the privilege of directly giving Congress the benefit of their views? A disturbing amount of the uproar over the Brannan Plan came from those who violently disapproved (or appeared to disapprove) the very idea of the Department's seeking to alter national farm policy through direct contact with Congress. The Farm Bureau, as we have seen, had a tendency to regard departmental policy recommendations as of dubious value (at least when they differed sharply from its own views!) because it felt that the major farm organizations were adequately equipped to represent the farmers and to supply Congress with policy proposals meeting the legitimate needs and aspirations of farm people. To acknowledge the value of major departmental policy innovations could be construed as a tacit admission of Bureau deficiencies in properly representing farmer interests, an admission not easily made.

Students of institutional behavior have long been aware that the leadership of large, well-established organizations promotes policies shaped in part by rank-and-file interests and pressures, but also reflecting the specialized knowledge, the power motives, and the bureaucratic tendencies of the ruling oligarchy. Whether or not the farm organizations faithfully represent the views of their members, however, is not the only question. Many farmers belong to no farm organization, and it may be seriously questioned whether they are being adequately represented. Furthermore, the various farm organizations frequently differ sharply among themselves as to the wisdom of alternative courses of public policy.

At any rate, Congress can make good use of suggestions from as many experienced and knowledgeable sources as possible. As argued earlier, the Department of Agriculture may well have perceptions, because of the nature of its responsibilities, which farm organizations cannot have. Furthermore, USDA's position as steward of the *public's* interest in agriculture normally predisposes it to more balanced viewpoints than can be expected from private groups. Thus the Department can often serve as both a positive legislative force and as a counterweight in resisting unjustified demands upon the government by farm organizations in their capacities as pressure groups.[3]

Some persons believe that administrators should not be encouraged to influence policy because of the tendencies of "bureaucrats" to constantly enlarge and deepen their sphere of activities. It could be argued with equal illogic that private pressure groups should be restrained from lobbying, since they have a propensity to ask for larger favors than the public interest will justify. Democracy, of course, posits the faith that Congress usually has sufficient judgment to recognize excesses and to blend conflicting and divergent views into a reasonably sound legislative product.

If we conclude that administrators have viewpoints which should be made available to Congress, and that there are reasonable doubts concerning both the representative character of institutional leadership and the breadth of perspective which private pressure groups can be expected to display, the proposition that the Department should "screen" its views through farm organizations, and abandon those meeting strong resistance, is effectively ruled out. If this practice were followed, the very recommendations which represent the national interest would sometimes be muffled or stifled.

This is not to say that Brannan was prudent in ignoring the Farm Bureau and the National Grange during the course of formulating his program. On the contrary, his failure to consult them was a first-class blunder. In this respect, the experience of the Brannan Plan can prove fruitful, for it has underscored a basic principle of administrative planning. That principle is that interested private groups should be sounded out and given an opportunity to work upon important Department policy proposals in advance of their public unveiling. The more drastic the changes being contemplated, the more imperative the necessity for such consultation.

Given the chance to participate in a Department's planning program, private organizations can often make searching criticisms and contribute constructive suggestions. They can also, where this proves desirable, more easily shift their own policy positions and prepare their membership for those shifts. But the ever-present problem of maintaining organizations' pride and status becomes well-nigh insoluble when a full-blown program receiving nationwide publicity is suddenly dropped in their laps. The chairman of the House Committee on Agriculture, Harold Cooley, realized this when he warned Brannan before the latter delivered his initial testimony that his Plan would receive rough treatment from the leading farm organizations because they had had no part in its formulation.[4]

If the Cabinet officer makes proposals clearly in line with the philosophy and general objectives of an organization, it can preserve its prestige by contending that the government is finally coming around to its point of view. But if this can not be demonstrated, or if there is latent hostility to the Secretary, a negative or even destructive attitude is likely to boil up.

It can be argued that the Farm Bureau and the Grange would have rejected out of hand Brannan's proposals, and that conferences with them prior to April 7, 1949, would have been fruitless. This is doubtless true, so far as Brannan's income support standard and 1800-unit rule are concerned, but it is entirely possible that the Bureau would have adopted a more friendly approach toward the direct payments–free market approach, in areas where price supports posed the greatest problems, had the Bureau not been presented with the Brannan Plan as a *fait accompli*.[5]

Apparently Brannan was more interested in reddening the Bureau's face than in saving it.[6] He is said to have believed that the time was ripe for a vital thrust at the Bureau, with its discomfiture redounding to the interests of the Department and the Farmers Union. If Brannan had first tried to broaden the area of agreement between himself and the Bureau, any subsequent shriveling of Bureau prestige would have come about in accordance with the rules of the game. But in inviting open combat before diplomacy was attempted, the principal casualty proved to be the public interest.

A further issue is involved in departmental participation in the making of public policy. Granting that a department has the right and obligation to make recommendations to Congress, has it also the right and obligation to fight for them? Should it advocate as well as originate? Or should it offer its legislative menu and humbly retire from the field, leaving Congress (in conjunction with representatives of the private pressure groups) to accept or reject its proposals without further pressure—direct or indirect—from the department?

And if a department—in this case the USDA—chooses to fight for its program, should it do so in co-operation with a political party, thus "plunging agricultural policy-making into partisan politics?"

The Farm Bureau, National Grange, almost all Republicans in the 81st Congress, and many Democrats answered the latter with an emphatic "no." They were convinced that farm policy must be bipartisan. Throwing the farm program into "politics" was regarded as inherently sinful, contrary to the farmers' best interests, and destructive of the public welfare.

Agricultural policy, however, has no more claim to being sheltered from partisan politics than does public policy affecting labor, business, or any other segment of the nation. Hence, if it is maintained that agricultural policy should be formulated on a nonpartisan basis, that conclusion logically represents a general conviction that parties should concern themselves with elections, with organization of the Congress, and with patronage, but not with important matters of public policy.

Party responsibility in matters of public policy is a question in itself, but the Brannan Plan concerns party behavior so directly that this question can not be sidestepped entirely.

Agricultural policy now is shaped almost exclusively by the agricultural committees of House and Senate.[7] Rarely are committee proposals radically altered or rejected in the chamber in which they originate (if the House of Representatives' action on agricultural policy in 1958 is excepted!). Membership of these committees, moreover, is mostly made up of Senators or Representatives from predominantly rural states or districts. Agricultural policy vitally affects the welfare of nonfarmers, yet representatives of the latter have little to say about the formulation of that policy. We have, in effect, one segment of the nation regulating and subsidizing itself.

Once made, this statement needs qualification. Many members serving on the Congressional agricultural committees are genuinely solicitous of the interests of nonfarmers. All points of view are usually brought out in committee hearings. The whole body of Senators and Representatives act in some sense as a moderating influence upon the committees. The President is in a position to veto flagrant class legislation. Finally, the agricultural committees have learned in recent years that farm policy must be drafted with greater respect for urban views if it is to stand much chance of being approved.

Yet when all of these factors are given their proper weight, the stubborn fact remains that agricultural legislation which is evolved on a nonpartisan basis uncomfortably approximates legislation for a minority by a minority.[8] No doubt such a procedure ordinarily protects very well the interests of agriculture, or at least the dominant elements within agriculture. But whether this institutional arrangement adequately protects the poorer farmers and non-farmers is open to serious question.

As E. A. Duddy wrote in 1932: "I do not agree . . . that agriculture alone must develop the agricultural policy of the U.S. It is a national problem, a national responsibility, a national policy, and all national policies must represent the combined thinking and discussion of all the people in the nation." [9]

In a two-party system, parties must of necessity serve (or give the impression of serving) the interests of all the people. In the struggle for survival and power, they ignore the legitimate claims of any important group or interest at their own peril, since the aggrieved minority may contribute the margin of defeat in the next election. Similarly, they expose themselves to danger if they yield to exorbitant demands by any minority group. By instinct, therefore, political parties tend to look upon issues with a wholeness that less inclusive political institutions can rarely match. Yet our political parties have evolved no satisfactory process by which party leadership can be adequately developed, recognized, and disciplined to the job of selecting and effectively supporting major legislative policies which are in the national interest. Because of this, farm-oriented agricultural committees receive remarkably little guidance from party leaders whose position would predispose them to a greater breadth of outlook than Congressional committees can normally command.

The inborn tendency of political parties in a two-party system to appraise proposed public policies from a many-sided view is a potentially valuable characteristic which can be suppressed only at a price. Certainly many of the nation's ills persist or are aggravated because they are dealt with from too parochial an outlook. The sensitivity of modern society to disturbances in any of its parts calls for decision-making by a political unit which is organically concerned with all of those parts. The metamorphosis, therefore, of American political parties into effective guardians of the balanced interests of the nation is a foremost national need.

The bold entrance of political parties into major aspects of policy-making would promote greater public interest in, and public understanding of, national legislative affairs. Party responsibility would correct what is perhaps the gravest weakness in our democratic system: it would clarify the political process; it would make comprehensible and coherent what is now a swirling confusion of power dispersion and irresponsibility.[10] A democracy must never forget that what the people cannot understand they cannot properly judge. Any movement or any decision, therefore, which tends to bring order, clarity, and responsibility out of the fog which swathes the formulation of national public policy should be welcomed by all who believe in government by the informed consent of the people.

Individual Congressmen tend to fall into public favor or disfavor largely because of the public's appraisal of their party's over-all performance. But it is almost impossible for the bewildered voter to make an accurate appraisal of that performance because parties usually have neither the leadership, the discipline, nor the will to plan a legislative program and assume responsibility for carrying it out. Perhaps the nature of the American system precludes firm party responsibility, but it may be devoutly hoped it does not preclude modest steps towards a political system which is not beyond the capacity of the average voter to understand—and therefore to judge.

Brannan may have erred in saying: "I want to confess . . . that I *do* think there should be and *is* such a thing as Party responsibility. I am also under the impression that the people have devised a political system for the purpose of self-government." [11] His opponents, however, have failed to point out wherein the error lay. Repetition of the cliché that agricultural policy should "stay out of politics" is no substitute for rational argument.

It cannot be said that Democratic party sponsorship of the Brannan Plan brought very encouraging results.[12] But it would be a mistake to draw too many pessimistic conclusions from this isolated and highly abnormal example. The Brannan Plan failed because it was conceived apart from most of the groups it affected, because it offered too much, and because American parties are far from being organized along lines enabling them to fulfill their proper function. It can well be argued that this was not the right program for a party endorsement, or not the right way to bring about greater party responsibility. But this is an altogether different proposition from charging that political parties should steer clear of direct involvement in agricultural policy-making.

Should a federal department serve as a public pressure group on behalf of the interests it serves? As a leading aspect of this question, is the Department of Agriculture ever justified in

seeking to enlarge (or maintain) federal bounties or services provided for a special segment of the nation? [13] The answer is yes,
but not an unqualified yes.

The Department has a responsibility to advance the legitimate interests of those it serves, whether those interests require
an enlargement or a diminution of government. But the Department's work should be done within a framework of directive
principles based upon a theory of government.

Ours is a highly organized nation. There is an organization to
represent almost every interest in society. Some of them are
remarkably effective in achieving their purposes. Others are so
poorly organized or unorganized that they are at an appalling
disadvantage in pressing for equal treatment and equal opportunities. Among these are white-collar workers, unorganized factory workers, and poverty-stricken classes in agriculture.

Concerning the latter, we have already cited Professor Hardin's statement that governmental agricultural policy "is largely
designed and administered for the benefit of commercial farmers." Hardin has also written: "Are low-income farmers a sepa-
rate force to be reckoned with in elections? Not so far." He
adds: "Low-income farmers as such have no effective pressure
groups at present." [14] On the other hand, the nation's commercial farmers are highly organized, with skillful and aggressive
representation in Washington. They are well equipped to de-
fend their interests and to exact at least those favors from government which are not adverse to the public welfare.

This suggests a major hypothesis. Public policy must inevitably adapt itself to the variety, intensity, and character of the
pressures made upon it. But it is essential that government be
an independent political force rather than the mere tool of
organized interests. If government yields to the organized pressures brought to bear upon it in proportion to their intensity
and persistence, it fails of its mission. It fails, in the first place,
to give the nation the leadership and vision which its position
uniquely enables it to provide. And if it merely reproduces the
existing power complex, on a different plane, its action can only
serve to exaggerate existing distortions. That is, the more power-

ful groups, through their control of government, will become ever stronger in relation to the weaker groups. They will have at their disposal a major instrument with which to extend the advantage which is already theirs.

Thus the government must adopt a different posture in dealing with the various groups composing society. The differentiation must be based not so much on "good" interests and "bad" interests, as upon the capacity for self-defense and aggression.

In questions involving the dominant interests, the role of government is fundamentally one of restraint. It must determine where legislative demands and nonlegislative activities spill over into the area of special privilege or represent predatory power drives. It must balance, refine, and moderate the claims of these powerful groups, whether those claims be against one another, against lesser groups in society, or against government itself.

In other instances, however, government should play a more affirmative part. It should try to insure, through positive measures if need be, that no group fails to share equitably in the benefits which government provides, or in the general advance of the people. It can often do this if it supplies the pressure which unorganized or weakly organized groups are unable to bring. Only through this compensatory action can all segments of our nation move forward in some kind of balanced proportion.

The Department of Agriculture, according to this concept, can rely upon the major farm organizations to ask enough for those they represent. In dealing with these dominant agricultural forces, the USDA must normally use its influence to hold back the reins, instead of applying the spurs. In the absence of party concern with agricultural legislation, this becomes all the more imperative.

Secretary Brannan never grasped this fundamental principle. On one occasion, he declared: "There may be reasonable differences as to where the level of support for farm income . . . should rest but I assure you that . . . I am afraid you are going to find me . . . erring on the high side." Again, he asserted: "I do not want to fool anybody. I am on the bullish side of farm prices; and if the Secretary of Agriculture is not, who is going to be?"

The only interpretation that can be put on the latter statement is that agricultural pressure groups are simply too timid to demand their share of government beneficence, and/or that they are not very effective lobbyists (which would be news to Congressmen!). Thus, the USDA must bolster them and even blaze the way in pleading for more than their self-sacrificial instincts will permit!

It was true, of course, that the National Grange and the Farm Bureau were not demanding one of the public favors which many of their members wanted—fixed, high-level, price supports.[15] This was a unique bit of good fortune for the USDA, and it posed a situation greatly simplifying the problems of Congress. Instead of sustaining these farm organizations in their moderation, however, Brannan proceeded to undermine their position. As a discerning politician, Brannan perceived what many (and perhaps most) commercial farmers wanted, and sought to give it to them in the form of a relatively inflexible formula of high-income supports.

In seeking ways to protect the income of producers of perishable commodities without penalizing the consumer, Brannan was admirably fulfilling one of his responsibilities as Secretary of Agriculture. He was acting as a spokesman for the American consumer—a highly unorganized and inarticulate class. For this he deserves full credit. In calling attention to the folly of ladling out large subsidies to our most prosperous farmers, he was also performing a valuable public service. But in leading the fight for price and income supports at unprecedented levels, he was guilty of precisely the error which the Department should avoid —outbidding powerful pressure groups in demands upon the public treasury.[16] In fairness to Brannan, it should be remembered that he regarded his income support standard as being in the larger interests of the entire nation. Unfortunately, his position was taken before careful soundings were made to determine whether his means would lead to the ends he sought.

The other half of the equation has been treated in the closing pages of Chapter III. With from one to one and one-half million farm families in the grip of numbing poverty, incapable of putting effective pressure on Congress, the USDA had a special responsibility on their behalf. It should have acted as their pressure group, not to demand mere largesse but to appeal for programs and policies which would help many of them improve their opportunities on the farm, or facilitate the movement of others to urban jobs.

These silent farm families which were receiving the crumbs that fell from the USDA's table might have had an aggressive champion in Charles F. Brannan. But the Secretary's preoccupation with the Brannan Plan, and later with high-level price supports, diverted him from this role for which he was so uniquely fitted. This was perhaps as great a misfortune as was the failure of Brannan's foes to recognize the creative vision which the Brannan Plan—at least in part—so clearly embodied.

NOTES

CHAPTER I

1. P.L. 897, 80th Cong., 2d Sess. (1948). The Agricultural Act of 1948 (sometimes referred to as the Hope-Aiken Act) consisted of two parts. Title I, fathered by Representative Clifford R. Hope (R–Kans.), continued price supports for a large number of farm commodities at 90 per cent of parity, with this protection expiring December 31, 1949. Title II, sponsored by Senator George D. Aiken (R–Vt.), was to become effective January 1, 1950. The latter initiated a system of flexible price supports ranging from 90 per cent to 60 per cent of parity, the support level being inversely related to the volume of supply.
2. U.S. Congress, House of Representatives, *General Farm Program,* Hearings before Committee on Agriculture, H.R., 81st Cong., 1st Sess. (Washington, 1949), Pt. 2, pp. 137–56.
3. *Economic Policy for American Agriculture,* pp. 28–29.
4. *A Balanced United States Agriculture in 1956,* National Planning Association Special Report No. 42, April, 1956.
5. *Farm Trouble* (Princeton, N.J.: Princeton University Press, 1957), p. 146.
6. *Ibid.,* p. 147.
7. *Policy for Commercial Agriculture,* Feb. 10, 1958, 85th Cong., 2d Sess. (Washington, 1958).
8. "Are Living Costs Out of Control?" *Atlantic,* February, 1957, p. 41.
9. "Farmers in a Changing World" (Washington, 1940), pp. 313 f.
10. Experience since World War II indicates that the farm surplus problem can no longer be attributed to unemployment and low levels of purchasing power. Technology is the major culprit today.
11. *Consumption of Food in the U.S., 1909–1948,* USDA Misc. Pub. 691, August, 1949.

12. On two previous occasions the Association of Land-Grant Colleges and Universities attempted a similar venture. The first was in 1927 and the second in 1932. John D. Black, "Land-Grant College Postwar Agricultural Policy," *Journal of Farm Economics*, February, 1945, p. 168.

13. *Journal of Farm Economics*, November, 1945, pp. 743 ff.

14. American Farm Economic Association, Committee on Parity Concepts, "On the Redefinition of Parity Price and Parity Income," *Journal of Farm Economics* (Proceedings Number), November, 1947, pp. 1358–77.

15. U.S. Congress, House of Representatives, *Postwar Economic Policy and Planning*, Hearings before Subcommittee on Agriculture and Mining, Special Subcommittee on Postwar Economic Policy and Planning, 78th Cong., 2d Sess., and 79th Cong., 1st Sess. (Washington, 1945), Pt. 5, pp. 1227–1305.

16. John D. Black, "The Bureau of Agricultural Economics—The Years in Between," *Journal of Farm Economics* (Proceedings Number), November, 1947, p. 1036.

17. U.S. Congress, House of Representatives, *Long-Range Agricultural Policy*, Hearings before Committee on Agriculture, H.R., 80th Cong., 1st Sess. (Washington, 1947), Pt. 1, pp. 2–12; and U.S. Congress, Senate, *Long-Range Agricultural Policy*, Hearings before Subcommittee of the Committee on Agriculture and Forestry, Senate, and the Committee on Agriculture, H.R., 80th Cong., 1st Sess. (Washington, 1948), pp. 2–222.

18. U.S. Congress, House of Representatives, *Postwar Economic Policy and Planning (Summary and Conclusions)*, Tenth Report of the House Special Committee on Postwar Economic Policy and Planning, 79th Cong., 2d Sess., House Report No. 2728.

19. *New York Times*, October 13, 1948, p. 18, col. 6.

20. P.L. 806, 80th Cong., 2d Sess. (1948).

21. *The American Farm Bureau Federation Official Newsletter*, January 5, 1949, p. 3.

22. Clifford R. Hope (R–Kans.), ranking Republican member of the House Committee on Agriculture. (*Congressional Record*, 81st Cong., 1st Sess., Vol. 95, Pt. 16, p. A5917.)

23. Senator George D. Aiken (R–Vt.), ranking Republican member of the Senate Committee on Agriculture and Forestry. (*Congressional Record*, 81st Cong., 1st Sess., Vol. 95, Pt. 3, p. 4031.)

24. Rep. Noah M. Mason (R–Ill.). (*Congressional Record*, 81st Cong., 2d Sess., Vol. 96, Pt. 5, p. 7167.)

25. Bryant Edwards, president, Texas and Southwest Cattle Raisers Association. (U.S. Congress, Senate, *Agricultural Adjustment Act of 1949*, Hearing before Subcommittee of the Committee on Agriculture and Forestry, U.S. Senate, 81st Cong., 1st Sess., on S. 1882 and S. 1971 [Washington, 1949], p. 337.)

26. E. H. Collins, *New York Times,* September 13, 1950, p. 36.

27. James G. Patton, president, National Farmers' Union, *National Union Farmer,* May, 1949, p. 8.

28. Information obtained during interviews with Senator Clinton P. Anderson (D–N. Mex.), Ralph S. Trigg, and Claude Wickard.

29. Interview with Senator Anderson.

30. *New York Times,* September 28, 1949, Part VI, p. 10.

31. In assuming this role, Brannan bore out the prediction of Senator Anderson. The latter has written, in connection with the selection of his successor: "I told the President that if he wanted a . . . Department of Agriculture that would back him and fight for the things he was fighting for, even to political support in the election, he would be better off with Mr. Brannan than with Edward Dodd, an alternative selection." (In a letter to me, September 24, 1952.) Perhaps it should be mentioned that Dodd accepted a position with the Food and Agriculture Organization of the United Nations, thereby leaving the way more directly open for Brannan's appointment.

32. *New York Times,* September 28, 1949, Part VI, p. 10.

33. *New York Times,* November 19, 1948, p. 16, col. 4.

34. *Ibid.*

35. USDA Press Release 2602–48, p. 11.

36. U.S. Congress, House of Representatives, *General Farm Program,* Hearings before Committee on Agriculture, H.R., 81st Cong., 1st Sess. (Washington, 1949), Pt. 2, pp. 184 f.

37. USDA Press Release 639–50.

38. U.S. Congress, Senate, *Long-Range Agricultural Policy,* Hearing before a Subcommittee of the Committee on Agriculture and Forestry, U.S. Senate, and the Committee on Agriculture, House of Representatives, 80th Cong., 1st Sess. (Washington, 1948), p. 162.

39. Information given me during an interview.

40. U.S. Congress, Senate, *Long-Range Agricultural Policy,* Hearings before a Subcommittee of the Committee on Agriculture and Forestry, U.S. Senate and the Committee on Agriculture, House of Representatives, 80th Cong., 1st Sess. (Washington, 1948), p. 4.

41. *New York Times,* May 25, 1948, p. 39, col. 5.

42. *New York Times,* July 4, 1948, p. 18, col. 1.

43. Information concerning the seminar and the planning session which followed was obtained by interviews with Wesley McCune, O. V. Wells, Ralph S. Trigg, John Baker, Frank Woolley, Philip F. Aylesworth, Maurice DuMars, Louis Bean, and Charles F. Brannan.

44. The omitted sections do not qualify or modify any of these points, but are either familiar generalities or peripheral suggestions.

45. Strangely, leading members of the seminar did not recall, when ques-

tioned, that the Secretary had sketched the Brannan Plan in broad outline during the seminar sessions.

46. Mr. McCune was already the author of two exceptionally readable books: *The Farm Bloc* (Garden City, New York: Doubleday-Doran & Co., 1943); and *The Nine Young Men* (New York: Harper & Bros., 1947).

47. Frank Woolley, Edward Shulman, and W. Carroll Hunter joined the working group from time to time to work on selected problems.

48. As gleaned from interviews with members of the working group.

49. In this connection, see also colloquy between Brannan and Rep. Stephen Pace (D–Ga.) on April 26, 1949. U.S. Congress, House of Representatives, *General Farm Program,* Hearings before Committee on Agriculture, H.R., 81st Cong., 1st Sess. (Washington, 1949), Pt. 2, p. 349.

50. Committee on Parity Concepts, American Farm Economic Association, "On the Redefinition of Parity Price and Parity Income," in O. B. Jesness (ed.), *Readings on Agricultural Policy* (Philadelphia: Blakiston, 1949), p. 220.

51. In his Congressional testimony, Brannan implied as much. U.S. Congress, House of Representatives, *General Farm Program,* Hearings before Committee on Agriculture, H.R., 81st Cong., 1st Sess. (Washington, 1949), Pt. 2, p. 180. Questioned on this point, Mr. Wells proved hard to pin down.

52. Wells was also on record as favoring "moderate" levels of support and "considerable flexibility . . . preferably at the administrative level." Committee on Parity Concepts, American Farm Economic Association, "On the Redefinition of Parity Price and Parity Income," in O. B. Jesness, *op. cit.*, p. 221.

53. Interview with Senator Anderson.

54. Wesley McCune has pointed out that "even the so-called inflexible supports flex monthly as the new parity ratio is calculated." The use of the term "inflexible," however, in connection with Brannan's income and price support levels, is consistent with the ordinary usage of the term in agricultural and journalistic circles. The violence of Brannan's attack on "flexible" supports, as that term is ordinarily used, should make this point clear.

55. *Congressional Record,* 81st Cong., 1st Sess., Vol. 95, Pt. 15, p. A4557. The subsequent survey of antecedents of the Brannan Plan is intended to be illustrative rather than comprehensive.

56. Committee on Parity Concepts, American Farm Economic Association, "On the Redefinition of Parity Price and Parity Income," in O. B. Jesness, *op. cit.*

57. In Jesness, *op. cit.*, the following endorse direct payments under some

circumstances for maintenance of farm income at desirable levels: O. B. Jesness, Professor of Agricultural Economics, University of Minnesota, p. 45; Geoffrey Shepherd, Professor of Agricultural Economics, Iowa State University, p. 161; Professor William H. Nicholls (winner of the essay contest sponsored by the American Farm Economic Association), p. 167; D. Gale Johnson, Assistant Professor of Economics, University of Chicago, p. 266; and the Committee on Parity Concepts of the American Farm Economic Association, p. 207. Other distinguished economists voicing similar sentiments included: John D. Black, Professor of Economics, Harvard University (Black and M. E. Kiefer, *Future Food and Agriculture Policy* [New York: McGraw-Hill Book Co., 1948], p. 214); and T. W. Schultz, Professor of Economics, University of Chicago (*Agriculture in an Unstable Economy* [New York: McGraw-Hill Co., 1945], pp. 221 ff.). Commenting on the manuscripts submitted in the *Journal of Farm Economics* essay contest, Chester C. Davis observed: "Among the prize-winning papers—eighteen in all—there was a strong accent on . . . government supplementary payments to maintain total returns from individual products or total over-all farm income." ("The Price Policy for Agriculture Contest," *Journal of Farm Economics,* November, 1945, p. 740.)

58. Report of the Committee on Parity Concepts, American Farm Economic Association, "Outline of a Price Policy for American Agriculture for the Postwar Period," *Journal of Farm Economics,* February, 1946, p. 133.

59. *Ibid.*

60. "At Farm Policy Hearings," *Farm Policy Forum,* January, 1948, p. 69.

61. National Planning Association, *Dare Farmers Risk Abundance?,* Planning Pamphlet No. 56 (Washington, February, 1947), p. 33.

62. U.S. Congress, Senate, *Agricultural Adjustment Act of 1949,* Hearing before Subcommittee of the Committee on Agriculture and Forestry, U.S. Senate, 81st Cong., 1st Sess. on S. 1882 and S. 1971 (Washington, 1949), p. 55.

63. Dairy Industry Committee, "Recommendations of the Dairy Industry Committee on Government Price Support of Dairy Products" (Washington, September, 1945), p. 1.

64. Report of Resolutions Committee, Tenth Constitutional Convention of CIO, Portland, Oregon, November 22–26, 1948, p. 17. This resolution reportedly represents the influence of Donald Montgomery, then Director of the Washington Office of the United Auto Workers. Mr. Montgomery, who was on friendly terms with Brannan, was formerly Consumer Counsel for the AAA.

65. Hardin, "The Bureau of Agricultural Economics Under Fire," p. 653.

66. U.S. Congress, House of Representatives, *Postwar Economic Policy and*

Planning, Tenth Report of the House Special Committee on Postwar Economic Policy and Planning, H. Report 2728, 79th Cong., 2d Sess., p. 40.

67. See John D. Black, "Evolution of Parity," in O. B. Jesness, *op. cit.,* p. 98.

68. *Congressional Record,* 81st Cong., 1st Sess., Vol. 95, Pt. 3, p. 4032.

69. Milton Eisenhower, "We Need a Conservation Policy That Works," *Farm Policy Forum,* October, 1948, p. 14.

70. Committee on Parity Concepts, American Farm Economic Association, "On the Redefinition of Parity Price and Parity Income," in O. B. Jesness, *op. cit.,* p. 215.

71. Black and Kiefer, *Future Food and Agriculture Policy,* p. 216.

72. U.S. Congress, Senate, *Long-Range Agricultural Policy and Program,* Hearing before Subcommittee of the Committee on Agriculture and Forestry, U.S. Senate, 80th Cong., 1st Sess., pursuant to S. Res. 147 (Washington, 1948), Pt. 1, p. 227.

73. H. H. Bennett, "Development of Natural Resources: The Coming Technological Revolution on the Land," *Science,* January 3, 1947 (condensed in *Farm Policy Forum,* October, 1948, p. 1).

74. Charles M. Hardin, *The Politics of Agriculture: Soil Conservation and the Struggle for Power in Rural America* (Glencoe, Illinois: The Free Press, 1952), p. 250.

75. Black and Kiefer, *Future Food and Agriculture Policy,* p. 238.

76. Committee on Parity Concepts, American Farm Economic Association, "On the Redefinition of Parity Price and Parity Income," in O. B. Jesness, *op. cit.,* p. 215.

77. "Agricultural Economists' Views on Farm Price Policy," *Journal of Farm Economics,* May, 1946, pp. 604 f.

78. *National Union Farmer,* May, 1949, p. 8.

79. U.S. Congress, House of Representatives, *Long-Range Agricultural Policy,* Hearings before Committee on Agriculture, H.R., 80th Cong., 1st Sess. (Washington, 1947), Pt. 2, p. 145.

80. *Ibid.,* p. 159.

81. U.S. Congress, Senate, *Agricultural Act of 1948,* Hearings before Committee on Agriculture and Forestry, U.S. Senate, 80th Cong., 2d Sess., on S. 2318 (Washington, 1948), p. 112.

82. *Ibid.,* p. 122.

83. U.S. Congress, House of Representatives, *Long-Range Agricultural Policy,* Hearings before Committee on Agriculture, H.R., 80th Cong., 1st Sess. (Washington, 1947), Pt. 2, p. 161.

84. Wilcox, *The Farmer in the Second World War* (Ames, Iowa: Iowa State Press, 1947), p. 382.

85. U.S. Congress, House of Representatives, *Postwar Economic Policy and Planning,* Hearings before Subcommittee on Agriculture and Mining, Special Subcommittee on Postwar Economic Policy and Planning, H.R., 78th Cong., 2d Sess., and 79th Cong., 1st Sess. (Washington, 1945), Pt. 5, p. 1546.

86. U.S. Congress, House of Representatives, *Long-Range Agricultural Policy,* Hearings before Committee on Agriculture, H.R., 80th Cong., 1st Sess. (Washington, 1947), Pt. 2, p. 146.

87. *Ibid.,* p. 148.

88. *Ibid.,* p. 152.

89. Records of the Democratic National Committee disclose that M. W. Thatcher, president of the Farmers Union Grain Terminal Association (the major component and recognized financial "angel" of the Farmers Union) contributed $2,500 to the Committee on November 24, 1948. Thatcher, incidentally, was one of the first major farm figures to come out for fixed, high-level price supports.

90. *New York Times,* November 20, 1948, p. 13, col. 1.

91. February, 1949, p. 8.

92. *Ibid.*

93. *Ibid.*

94. *Ibid.,* March, 1949.

95. National Planning Association, *Must We Have Food Surpluses?,* Planning Pamphlet No. 66, Agriculture Committee Report of the National Planning Association (Washington, March, 1949), p. 12.

96. *National Union Farmer,* May, 1949, p. 1.

97. *Ibid.,* p. 8.

98. At one point Brannan denied that anyone outside the Department was consulted during the formulating period. "For the protection of the professional standing of Mr. Schultz or anyone else outside the department, I would like to say that they have not been consulted about the program." U.S. Congress, House of Representatives, *General Farm Program,* Hearings before Committee on Agriculture, H.R., 81st Cong., 1st Sess. (Washington, 1949), Pt. 2, p. 179. While this is substantially correct, Professor Charles M. Hardin of the University of Chicago was present during part of March, 1949, knew what was going on, and contributed some suggestions to the Secretary's working group.

99. In this survey of the relationship between the Farmers Union and the Brannan Plan, mention should perhaps be made that John Baker, a long-time friend of Patton's, left the USDA in May, 1951, to become legislative representative of Patton's organization. Wesley McCune was also on very friendly terms with Patton and was partisan to the general views held by the Farmers Union. After leaving the Department in

1953, Brannan assumed the position of general counsel for the Farmers Union.

100. *New York Times,* November 18, 1949, p. 17, col. 1.

101. *American Farm Bureau Official Newsletter,* September 17, 1951, pp. 1–4.

102. *New York Times,* December 15, 1949, p. 6, col. 3.

103. Senator Anderson did not wholly subscribe to his own theory while serving as Secretary of Agriculture. The long-range testimony offered by USDA in 1947 contained some rather specific suggestions concerning the direction agricultural policy should take. While Anderson was certainly not as persistent or as aggressive as Brannan in pressing his views, he was not the self-abnegating administrator the above-cited quotation would indicate.

104. Chester C. Davis, "The Development of Agricultural Policy Since the End of the World War," *Farmers in a Changing World: 1940 Yearbook of Agriculture* (Washington, 1940), p. 316.

105. Madison: University of Wisconsin Press, 1950, p. 462.

106. Davis, *op. cit.,* p. 314.

107. Saloutos and Hicks, *op. cit.,* p. 460.

108. Interview with Mr. Aylesworth.

109. U.S. Congress, Senate, *Long-Range Agricultural Policy,* Hearings before a Subcommittee of the Committee on Agriculture and Forestry, U.S. Senate and the Committee on Agriculture, H.R., 80th Cong., 1st Sess., pursuant to S. Res. 147 and H. Res. 298 (Washington, 1948), p. 196.

110. *Congressional Record,* 81st Cong., 1st Sess., Vol. 96, Pt. 7, p. 9846.

111. *New York Times,* September 17, 1947, p. 23, col. 7.

CHAPTER II

1. U.S. Congress, House of Representatives, *General Farm Program,* Hearings before Committee on Agriculture, H.R., 81st Cong., 1st Sess. (Washington, 1949), Pt. 2, p. 138.

2. USDA Press Release 422–50, p. 5.

3. USDA Press Release 1702–50, p. 4.

4. O. B. Jesness, "Postwar Agricultural Policy—Pressure versus General Welfare," in O. B. Jesness, *op. cit.,* p. 48. See also *Congressional Record,* 81st Cong., 1st Sess., Vol. 95, Pt. 11, p. 14306.

5. As the controversy lengthened, however, Brannan tended more and more to attribute a unique importance to the role of farm income in sustaining prosperity.

6. USDA Press Release 1702–50, p. 11; and USDA Press Release 2651–49, pp. 1 f. See also Brannan's testimony before the Senate Committee on Agriculture and Forestry, July 7, 1949 (pp. 50–52 of the hearings).

7. USDA Press Release 1702–50, p. 11.

8. USDA Press Release 545–50, p. 3.

9. U.S. Congress, House of Representatives, *General Farm Program,* Hearings before Committee on Agriculture, H.R., 81st Cong., 1st Sess. (Washington, 1949), Pt. 2, p. 292.

10. U.S. Congress, Senate, *Agricultural Adjustment Act of 1949,* Hearing before Subcommittee of the Committee on Agriculture and Forestry, U.S. Senate, 81st Cong., 1st Sess., on S. 1882 and S. 1971 (Washington, 1949), p. 53.

11. USDA Press Release 545–50, p. 15.

12. USDA Press Release 422–50, p. 4.

13. *Ibid.,* p. 10.

14. U.S. Congress, Senate, *Agricultural Adjustment Act of 1949,* Hearing before Subcommittee of the Committee on Agriculture and Forestry, U.S. Senate, 81st Cong., 1st Sess., on S. 1882 and S. 1971 (Washington, 1949), p. 81.

15. T. W. Schultz, quoted in *Educational and Methods Conference in Public Policy,* The Farm Foundation, January, 1950, p. 53.

16. "An Analysis of the Brannan Plan," New York: Research Department, National Association of Manufacturers, October, 1949, p. 12.

17. *Ibid.,* p. 13.

18. *Ibid.*

19. U.S. Congress, Senate, *Agricultural Adjustment Act of 1949,* Hearing before Subcommittee of the Committee on Agriculture and Forestry, U.S. Senate, 81st Cong., 1st Sess., on S. 1882 and S. 1971 (Washington, 1949), p. 158.

20. *Ibid.,* pp. 159 f.

21. Schultz, *Production and Welfare of Agriculture* (New York: Macmillan Co., 1950), p. 183.

22. Schultz, *Agriculture in an Unstable Economy,* p. 159.

23. U.S. Congress, House of Representatives, *General Farm Program,* Hearings before Committee on Agriculture, H.R., 81st Cong., 1st Sess. (Washington, 1949), Pt. 3, p. 524. It is interesting to note that wheat producers and storage men, acting through the Farmers Union Grain Terminal Association and the Farmers Union, were in the forefront of the campaign to exterminate the "sliding scale."

24. Schultz, *Agriculture in an Unstable Economy,* pp. 10–12.

25. Walter W. Wilcox, *Social Responsibility in Farm Leadership* (New York: Harper & Bros., 1956), p. 29.

26. U.S. Congress, Senate, *Agricultural Adjustment Act of 1949,* Hearing

before Subcommittee of the Committee on Agriculture and Forestry, U.S. Senate, 81st Cong., 1st Sess., on S. 1882 and S. 1971 (Washington, 1949), p. 162.

27. U.S. Congress, House of Representatives, *General Farm Program,* Hearings before Committee on Agriculture, H.R., 81st Cong., 1st Sess. (Washington, 1949), Pt. 2, p. 151.

28. Brannan freely conceded, when questioned by the chairman of the House Agricultural Committee, that commodity controls are an essential complement of high support prices. *Ibid.,* p. 268.

29. California State Agricultural Extension Service, *Economics Brief for California Agricultural Extension Personnel* (Berkeley, California, April 25, 1950), p. 94.

30. Since I am not a sociologist, I will not evaluate the charge made by a state Farm Bureau president that the Brannan Plan would eventually lead to miscegenation!

31. This information was obtained during an interview with Mr. Woolley. Wesley McCune insists that O. V. Wells was responsible for drawing up the cost estimates.

32. *Congressional Record,* 81st Cong., 2d Sess., Vol. 96, Pt. 17, p. A5809. For Brannan's rebuttal, see his speech before the National Grange, November 19, 1949. USDA Press Release 2466–49, p. 9.

33. The USDA estimated in October, 1957, that a direct payments program covering twenty-six major commodities supported at 90 per cent parity would cost about seven billion dollars under a controlled production program, and up to ten billion dollars under an uncontrolled program. Since Brannan proposed direct payments for only a handful of commodities, however, the USDA estimate has little relevance to this study.

34. U.S. Congress, House of Representatives, *General Farm Program,* Hearings before Committee on Agriculture, H.R., 81st Cong., 1st Sess. (Washington, 1949), Pt. 2, p. 212.

35. *Ibid.,* p. 210.

36. *Ibid.,* p. 211.

37. U.S. Congress, Senate, *Agricultural Adjustment Act of 1949,* Hearing before Subcommittee of the Committee on Agriculture and Forestry, U.S. Senate, 81st Cong., 1st Sess., on S. 1882 and S. 1971 (Washington, 1949), p. 54.

38. U.S. Congress, House of Representatives, *General Farm Program,* Hearings before Committee on Agriculture, H.R., 81st Cong., 1st Sess. (Washington, 1949), Pt. 2, p. 209.

39. "Capitol Cloak Room," Columbia Broadcasting System, July 20, 1949.

40. U.S. Congress, House of Representatives, *General Farm Program,* Hearings before Committee on Agriculture, H.R., 81st Cong., 1st Sess. (Washington, 1949), Pt. 2, p. 219.

41. The income support standard approximated 100 per cent of old parity under Title I of the Agricultural Act of 1948, 100 per cent of modernized parity in Title II of the same Act, and from 90 per cent of parity for crops under the revisions of the Agricultural Act of 1949 to 100 per cent of parity on livestock. John K. Rose, *The Brannan Plan*, Public Affairs Bulletin No. 78, Legislative Reference Service, Library of Congress, April, 1950, p. 42. However, since the forward movement of the base period would cause the replacement of low income prewar years with high income postwar years, the support standard would climb another 5 per cent to 6 per cent within a few years.

42. U.S. Congress, Senate, *Agricultural Adjustment Act of 1949*, Hearing before Subcommittee of the Committee on Agriculture and Forestry, U.S. Senate, 81st Cong., 1st Sess., on S. 1882 and S. 1971 (Washington, 1949), p. 162.

43. *Des Moines Register*, February 16, 1950, p. 10.

44. Oscar Heline and Donald R. Kaldor, Planning Pamphlet No. 72 (Washington: National Planning Association, July, 1950), p. 41.

45. U.S. Congress, *Policy for Commercial Agriculture*, Hearings before the Subcommittee on Agricultural Policy of the Joint Economics Committee, 85th Cong., 1st Sess., p. 300.

46. *Des Moines Register*, p. 10.

47. Heline and Kaldor, *op. cit.*, p. 63. Analysis of Mr. Patton's argument will be delayed until certain basic facts can be established at a later point in the chapter.

48. *Congressional Record*, 81st Cong., 2d Sess., Vol. 96, Pt. 17, p. A5809.

49. U.S. Congress, House of Representatives, *General Farm Program*, Hearings before Committee on Agriculture, H.R., 81st Cong., 1st Sess. (Washington, 1949), Pt. 2, p. 216.

50. USDA Press Release 1951–52, p. 2.

51. *Congressional Record*, 81st Cong., 2d Sess., Vol. 96, Pt. 17, p. A5809.

52. Although the Farmers Union has become the foremost advocate of 100 per cent of parity price supports, James G. Patton declared in 1947 that "Ninety per cent of parity price supports might force us into a completely managed agricultural economy." U.S. Congress, Senate, *Long-Range Agricultural Policy and Program*, Hearings before a Subcommittee of the Committee on Agriculture and Forestry, U.S. Senate, 80th Cong., 1st Sess., pursuant to S. Res. 147 (Washington, 1948), Pt. V, p. 12.

53. John K. Rose, *The Brannan Plan*, Public Affairs Bulletin No. 78, April, 1950, p. 48.

54. USDA Press Release 422–50, p. 8.

55. U.S. Congress, House of Representatives, *General Farm Program*, Hearings before Committee on Agriculture, H.R., 81st Cong., 1st Sess. (Washington, 1949), Pt. 2, p. 249. See also Heline and Kaldor, *op. cit.*, p. 61.

56. Dale E. Hathaway and Lawrence W. Witt, "Agricultural Policy: Whose Valuations?" *Journal of Farm Economics,* August, 1952, pp. 299 ff.

57. *Ibid.,* pp. 305 f.

58. U.S. Congress, *Policy for Commercial Agriculture,* Hearings before the Subcommittee, 85th Cong., 1st Sess., p. 299.

59. Wilcox, "Comments on Agricultural Policy," p. 812.

60. D. Gale Johnson, *Trade and Agriculture, op. cit.* p. 88 (footnote).

61. *Congressional Record,* 81st Cong., 1st Sess., Vol. 95, Pt. 11, p. 14311.

62. Perhaps the most impressive description of the administrative problems involved in production payments was made by Mark W. Pickell, Executive Secretary, Corn Belt Livestock Feeders Association. See U.S. Congress, House of Representatives, *General Farm Program,* Hearings before Committee on Agriculture, H.R., 81st Cong., 1st Sess. (Washington, 1949), Pt. 6, pp. 1180 ff.

63. New York: John Wiley and Sons, 1950, p. 91. For a different view, see Wilcox, *Social Responsibility in Farm Leadership,* p. 37.

64. Information obtained through inquiries at the State Department.

65. "Long-Run Effects of Price-Maintenance Policy for Agricultural Products," in O. B. Jesness, *op. cit.,* p. 223. See also Schultz, *Agriculture in an Unstable Economy,* p. 37; and Johnson, *Trade and Agriculture,* p. 85.

66. *Who's Behind Our Farm Policy?* (New York: Frederick A. Praeger, 1956), p. 174.

67. U.S. Congress, House of Representatives, *General Farm Program,* Hearings before Committee on Agriculture, H.R., 81st Cong., 1st Sess. (Washington, 1949), Pt. 2, p. 222.

68. "The Bureau of Agricultural Economics Under Fire: A Study in Valuation Conflicts," *Journal of Farm Economics,* August, 1946.

69. Charles M. Hardin, "Programmatic Research and Agricultural Policy," *Journal of Farm Economics,* May, 1947, p. 373. See also p. 362.

70. The over-all economic returns of part-time farmers was not known, but Professor Black has testified that 30 per cent of New England farmers were part-time farmers, and that if one adds their off-the-farm income, they enjoy higher than average over-all incomes. U.S. Congress, Senate, *Agricultural Adjustment Act of 1949,* Hearing before Subcommittee of the Committee on Agriculture and Forestry, U.S. Senate, 81st Cong., 1st Sess., on S. 1882 and S. 1971 (Washington, 1949), p. 161.

71. U.S. Department of Commerce, *Survey of Current Business,* July, 1952, Table 26, p. 22.

72. U.S. Congress, Senate, *Agricultural Adjustment Act of 1949,* Hearing before Subcommittee of the Committee on Agriculture and Forestry, U.S. Senate, 81st Cong., 1st Sess., on S. 1882 and S. 1971 (Washington, 1949), p. 161.

73. Government may be properly concerned with a fair return if current returns are so low that needed productive resources are not being properly utilized or developed. This situation, however, does not threaten American agriculture.

74. *A Joint Statement on Farm Policy*, National Planning Association, Special Report No. 40, January, 1956.

75. In 1956, noncommercial farm families earned $2,925 from all sources, commercial farm families $5,415, and nonfarm families $6,900. *Policy for Commercial Agriculture*, Report of the Subcommittee on Agricultural Policy to the Joint Economic Committee, 85th Cong., 2d Sess., p. 5.

76. National Planning Association, Planning Pamphlet No. 77 (Washington, January, 1952), p. 5.

77. It will be noted that the term "commercial farm" as used by agricultural economists differs from the usage employed by the Census Bureau. The latter refers to all farms run by full-time operators as "commercial farms," whereas agricultural economists customarily refer to the 45 per cent of American farms which produce about 90 per cent of the farm commodities as "commercial farms."

78. This figure adjusts for the 27 per cent increase in sales over census figures, as reported by BAE.

79. Charles M. Hardin, "The Politics of Agriculture in the United States," *Journal of Farm Economics*, November, 1950, p. 573.

80. Johnson, *Trade and Agriculture*, pp. 89 f.

81. *Social Responsibility in Farm Leadership*, p. 37.

82. These farmers would still receive protection on the first $25,000 worth of their sales.

83. It may be doubted that the family farm is being displaced by corporation-type farms. See J. D. Black, "The Future of the Family Farm," *Yale Review*, June, 1956.

84. U.S. Congress, House of Representatives, *General Farm Program*, Hearings before Committee on Agriculture, H.R., 81st Cong., 1st Sess. (Washington, 1949), Pt. 2, p. 337.

85. *Ibid.*, p. 341.

86. *Ibid.*, p. 233.

87. *Ibid.*, pp. 217 f. Brannan never completely abandoned his limitation principle, but he was apparently far more willing to sacrifice it than other features of his Plan. In this connection, it may be noted that several Congressmen suggested that Brannan's objective could be met by applying his limitation principle to acreage allotments. To this Brannan responded, "If the committee wants to go ahead and do this I am not suggesting that you do not." (!) *Ibid.*, p. 196.

88. The 1800-unit rule did not become a major point of controversy, con-

trary to Brannan's expectations. Some observers, however, think it engendered much greater hostility than surface indications would lead one to believe.

89. T. W. Schultz, "That Turbulent Brannan Plan," *Farm Policy Forum,* February, 1950, p. 5.
90. Schultz, *Production and Welfare of Agriculture,* p. 177.
91. D. Gale Johnson, "High Level Support Prices and Corn Belt Agriculture," *Journal of Farm Economics,* August, 1949, p. 519.
92. U.S. Congress, House of Representatives, *General Farm Program,* Hearings before Committee on Agriculture, H.R., 81st Cong., 1st Sess. (Washington, 1949), Pt. 2, p. 153.
93. U.S. Congress, Senate, *Agricultural Adjustment Act of 1949,* Hearing before Subcommittee of the Committee on Agriculture and Forestry, U.S. Senate, 81st Cong., 1st Sess., on S. 1882 and S. 1971 (Washington, 1949), p. 90.
94. *National Union Farmer,* November, 1949, p. 2.
95. Heline and Kaldor, *op. cit.,* p. 63.
96. USDA Press Release 2675-49. Mr. Brannan's program has since been largely adopted, on an experimental basis, by Ezra Taft Benson. It is called the Rural Development Program.
97. "Comments on Agricultural Policy," p. 806.
98. *Policy for Commercial Agriculture,* p. 7.
99. Program Committee of the Committee for Economic Development, *Toward a Realistic Farm Program,* December 1957, pp. 29 ff.
100. This should not be interpreted as a failure to recognize the necessity of maintaining national food and fiber reserves adequate for national emergencies.
101. That is, except among some agricultural economists and a few newspapers.
102. *Christian Agriculture,* January 15, 1950, p. 3.

CHAPTER III

1. John M. Vorys, "The Lobby That Taxes Built," *Nation's Business,* April, 1950, p. 42.
2. Charles M. Hardin, "The Politics of Conservation: An Illustration," *Journal of Politics,* August, 1951, p. 469.
3. James L. McCamy, *Government Publicity* (Chicago: University of Chicago Press, 1939), p. 15.
4. U.S. Congress, Senate, *Investigation of the Executive Agencies of the Government,* S. Report 1275 of the Select Committee to Investigate the

Executive Agencies of the Government, U.S. Senate, 75th Cong., 1st Sess. (Washington, 1937).

5. Junius B. Wood, "Ballyhoo Runs Wild," *Nation's Business,* July, 1945, p. 66.

6. *Ibid.,* p. 68.

7. *Ibid.*

8. "Propaganda Activities of Big Government Under Scrutiny," *Congressional Digest,* May, 1941, p. 135.

9. U.S. Congress, House of Representatives, *Investigation of AAA and PMA Publicity and Propaganda in Nebraska,* Report of Committee on Expenditures in the Executive Departments, H.R., 80th Cong., 1st Sess. (Washington, 1948), p. 1.

10. Forrest A. Harness, "Federal Thought Control," Supplement to *American Affairs,* Spring, 1948, p. 7.

11. Public Affairs Institute sent staff members to USDA to study the Plan, but since the working group came to entertain grave doubts as to the soundness of Brannan's proposals, no material was issued.

12. Information on the activities of state extension directors was obtained by means of a questionnaire which I circulated to all state directors.

13. These meetings covered the period from October, 1949, to January, 1951.

14. Several state directors contended that it was not their responsibility to carry on informational work about legislative proposals being considered by Congress. This attitude, however, was not shared by the overwhelming majority of directors.

15. One director volunteered the information that "while extension did send out some information, most of the information that went out dealing with this subject was prepared in our office, but distributed by PMA." He did not elaborate in what manner PMA made such distribution.

16. Hardin, "The Politics of Conservation," p. 473.

17. Charles M. Hardin, "Reflections on Agricultural Policy Formation in the United States," *American Political Science Review,* October, 1948, p. 884.

18. Hardin, "The Politics of Conservation," p. 469.

19. Both men had left USDA when interviewed on this matter.

20. Letter to state PMA chairmen, May 12, 1949.

21. Senator Aiken scored "Questions and Answers" as "purely and simply propaganda designed to promote a political plan of prosperity for American farmers. . . . If anyone can find in this document anything which is not purely political, I should like to have him point it out to me." *Congressional Record,* 81st Cong., 1st Sess., Vol. 95, Pt. 6, p. 7590. The Senator greatly overstated his case, although the document un-

questionably presents the Plan in a manner calculated to create a favorable impression. The last twenty-five questions, however, related strictly to the mechanics of the proposed program.

22. R. W. Davenport, "The Duchy of Brannan," *Fortune,* October, 1950, p. 47.

23. Hardin, *The Politics of Agriculture,* p. 30.

24. Washington PMA officials conceded that the state chairman of one Western state spent a substantial amount of time stumping the state on behalf of the Brannan Plan.

25. Most state committees apparently did not believe it was necessary or advisable to caution their county committeemen about propagandizing for the Plan. A few did so, however.

26. U.S. Congress, House of Representatives, *Legislative Activities of Executive Agencies,* Hearings before the House Select Committee on Lobbying Activities, H.R., 81st Cong., 2d Sess. (Washington, 1950), Pt. 10, pp. 82 f.

27. *Ibid.,* p. 191.

28. *Ibid.,* pp. 65–77.

29. *Congressional Record,* 81st Cong., 2d Sess., Vol. 96, Pt. 5, p. 5051.

30. *Ibid.,* pp. 5050 f.

31. The actual cost was $42,109. U.S. Congress, House of Representatives, *Legislative Activities of Executive Agencies,* Hearings before the House Select Committee on Lobbying Activities, H.R., 81st Cong., 2d Sess. (Washington, 1950), Pt. 10, p. 92.

32. *Congressional Record,* 81st Cong., 2d Sess., Vol. 96, Pt. 5, p. 5051.

33. U.S. Congress, House of Representatives, *Legislative Activities of Executive Agencies,* Hearings before the House Select Committee on Lobbying Activities, H.R., 81st Cong., 2d Sess. (Washington, 1950), Pt. 10, pp. 77–80.

34. *Congressional Record,* 81st Cong., 2d Sess., Vol. 96, Pt. 8, p. 9999.

35. *Ibid.,* pp. 9999 f.

36. For example, see the testimony of Roger W. Jones, Assistant Director, Bureau of the Budget, Division of Legislative Reference. U.S. Congress, House of Representatives, *Legislative Activities of Executive Agencies,* Hearings before House Select Committee on Lobbying Activities, H.R., 81st Cong., 2d Sess. (Washington, 1950), Pt. 10, p. 15.

37. U.S. Congress, House of Representatives, *The Role of Lobbying in Representative Self-Government,* Hearings before House Select Committee on Lobbying Activities, H.R., 81st Cong., 2d Sess. (Washington, 1950), Pt. 1, p. 159.

38. *Ibid.,* p. 16:.

39. U.S. Congress, House of Representatives, *Legislative Activities of Executive Agencies,* Hearings before House Select Committee on Lobbying

Activities, H.R., 81st Cong., 2d Sess. (Washington, 1950), Pt. 10, pp. 150 f.
It is of course natural that an Attorney General would be reluctant to
prosecute officials for promoting causes in which the President was
interested. To further insure the futility of 18 U.S. Code, 1913, the
Courts refuse to entertain any suit brought by a private citizen to
restrain the expenditure of duly appropriated funds. *Alabama Power
Co.* v. *Ickes, 302* U.S. 464.

40. On the basis of incomplete evidence, it appears that USDA under
Secretary Benson has engaged in much the same informational work as
it did under Brannan.

CHAPTER IV

1. Brannan, when I interviewed him, conceded that his support formula
resulted in tobacco prices somewhat higher than he believed desirable.
2. McCune, *The Farm Bloc,* p. 190.
3. A. G. Mezerik, "The Brannan Plan," *New Republic,* November 28,
1949, p. 11.
4. Stuart Chase, *Democracy Under Pressure* (New York: Twentieth Century Fund, 1945), p. 96.
5. Hardin, "The Politics of Agriculture in the United States," p. 573.
6. Roger Fleming, head of the Farm Bureau's Washington Office, once
described PMA as the number-one enemy of the Bureau. *Washington
Post,* December 12, 1949.
7. See p. 129.
8. Wilcox, *The Farmer in the Second World War,* p. 373.
9. *Ibid.,* p. 382. It might be noted that the Bureau and the Grange were
also opposed to price ceilings on farm products.
10. Johnson, *Trade and Agriculture,* p. 88.
11. U.S. Congress, House of Representatives, *General Farm Program,*
Hearings before Committee on Agriculture, H.R., 81st Cong., 1st Sess.
(Washington, 1949), Pt. 2, p. 290. See also *Congressional Record,* 81st
Cong., 1st Sess., Vol. 95, Pt. 10, p. 12776.
12. *Congressional Record,* 81st Cong., 1st Sess., Vol. 95, Pt. 3, p. 4032.
13. *Ibid.,* pp. 4031 f.
14. U.S. Congress, House of Representatives, *General Farm Program,* Hearings before Committee on Agriculture, H.R., 81st Cong., 1st Sess.
(Washington, 1949), Pt. 2, p. 166.
15. *Proceedings of National Farm Institute,* February 17–18, 1950, p. 95.
16. *The American Farm Bureau Federation Official Newsletter,* January 5,
1949; February 16, 1949; and March 14, 1949.
17. Quoted in USDA Press Release 422–50, p. 10.

18. Assuming an *effective* 1800-unit rule.

19. U.S. Congress, Senate, *Agricultural Adjustment Act of 1949*, Hearing before Subcommittee of the Committee on Agriculture and Forestry, U.S. Senate, 81st Cong., 1st Sess., on S. 1882 and S. 1971 (Washington, 1949), p. 208.

20. The Bureau had become accustomed to more deferential treatment. Professor Hardin has written: "remarks of Secretary Anderson strongly suggest that the staff work and advisory function in policy formulation have been transferred, not to his office, but to the research divisions of the national farm organizations, chiefly the American Farm Bureau Federation." Hardin, "The Bureau of Agricultural Economics Under Fire," p. 639.

21. U.S. Congress, Senate, *Agricultural Adjustment Act of 1949*, Hearing before Subcommittee of the Committee on Agriculture and Forestry, U.S. Senate, 81st Cong., 1st Sess., on S. 1882 and S. 1971 (Washington, 1949), p. 208.

22. Letter from Brannan to Joseph and Stewart Alsop (file copy undated).

23. *New York Times,* April 11, 1949, p. 2, col. 2. The Democratic National Committee publication, *Capital Comment,* devoted almost its entire issue of April 9, 1949 to Brannan's opening testimony. Frequently, thereafter, additional material appeared in this paper extolling the Plan and denouncing its critics.

24. USDA Press Release 422–50, pp. 12 f. Brannan's bitterness is explicable in view of the opinion expressed in a letter from Wesley McCune to Fowler V. Hamilton, New York, on February 10, 1950, that "Kline, perhaps more than any other man, is responsible for blocking our efforts to strengthen the price support legislation and make it workable by supplying the tools we must have to carry out price supports."

25. U.S. Congress, Senate, *Agricultural Adjustment Act of 1949*, Hearing before Subcommittee of the Committee on Agriculture and Forestry, U.S. Senate, 81st Cong., 1st Sess., on S. 1882 and S. 1971 (Washington, 1949), p. 272.

26. McCune indicates that the Master of the Grange had become disenchanted with flexible supports by 1955, and "suggested changes in farm policy along the lines of free market prices with supplementary government payments to farmers, as proposed by former Secretary Brannan." *Who's Behind Our Farm Policy?*, p. 36.

27. Brannan appeared quite willing to settle for fixed 90 per cent of parity price supports for storables as an alternative to his income support standard. Most of his speeches, in fact, belabored flexible supports rather than directly defended his support standard. Those who heard his speeches, incidentally, would never guess that Brannan was already authorized, under the Agricultural Act of 1948 (and later, under the

Agricultural Act of 1949) to maintain supports at 90 per cent of parity regardless of the supply situation. Brannan's refusal (except in committee) to give recognition to this vital fact aroused the ire of Senator Aiken. The latter felt Brannan was playing less than fair in vigorously campaigning for a power which was already his.

28. One qualification should be noted. Opponents of the Plan felt some uneasiness about concentrating the political attack upon production payments in view of market uncertainties. Brannan's foes knew full well that continued market declines, accompanied by heavy government purchases, would gravely weaken their case.

29. "Mr. Secretary, you have made a very splendid, forthright and comprehensive statement. I hope it will be read by all of the farmers of this country, and especially do I hope it will be read by the consumers of the country. I think you have in rather bold and brilliant fashion discussed the very perplexing problems that American agriculture is now facing." U.S. Congress, House of Representatives, *General Farm Program*, Hearings before Committee on Agriculture, H.R., 81st Cong., 1st Sess. (Washington, 1949), Pt. 2, p. 157.

30. U.S. Congress, House of Representatives, *General Farm Program*, Hearings before Committee on Agriculture, H.R., 81st Cong., 1st Sess. (Washington, 1949), Pt. 2, pp. 340 f.

31. "For two and a half years," Senator Anderson has written, "Mr. Patton had been regularly calling on the President urging him to kick me out and the President had become a little displeased with him because he did not feel that he wanted to be constantly told what a poor appointment he had made originally." (In a letter to me, September 24, 1952.)

32. I obtained this information during an interview with Senator Anderson.

33. Press Release, April 9, 1949.

34. *Congressional Record*, 81st Cong., 1st Sess., Vol. 95, Pt. 3, pp. 4031 f.

35. *Congressional Record*, 81st Cong., 1st Sess., Vol. 95, Pt. 6, p. 7592.

36. *Congressional Record*, 81st Cong., 2d Sess., Vol. 96, Pt. 10, p. 13338.

37. *Congressional Record*, 81st Cong., 1st Sess., Vol. 95, Pt. 7, p. 9844.

38. *Congressional Record*, 81st Cong., 1st Sess., Vol. 95, Pt. 7, p. 9841.

39. Further polling results are recorded in Rose, *The Brannan Plan*, pp. 69 f.

40. *New York Times*, May 14, 1950, p. 7, col. 6.

41. Hathaway and Witt, *op. cit.*

42. *New York Times*, August 21, 1952, p. 12, col. 6; September 7, 1952, p. 70, col. 7; September 19, 1952, p. 14, col. 3; and October 16, 1952, p. 23, col. 4.

43. "The Farm Policy Dilemma," *Journal of Farm Economics*, August, 1958, p. 569.

44. "A Modified Compensatory Price Program for Agriculture," *Journal of Farm Economics*, November, 1955, pp. 717–18.
45. *Farm Prices* (Minneapolis: University of Minnesota Press, 1958), pp. 163.

CHAPTER V

1. Alternative views regarding the proper general relationship of administrators to public planning are well summarized in Leonard D. White, *Introduction to the Study of Public Administration* (New York: The Macmillan Co., 1948), p. 227.
2. V. O. Key has made the point: "Within the administrative service of the Government there is a much greater tendency to seek to promote the public welfare as a whole through new legislation than will be found in the ranks of leaders of private pressure groups." V. O. Key, *Politics, Parties and Pressure Groups* (New York: Crowell Co., 1942), p. 179.
3. *Ibid.*, p. 379. If it is contended that the price-support levels proposed by the Brannan Plan do not sustain this generalization, the answer is that Brannan's position was exceptional rather than typical of USDA Secretaries; conversely, the self-restraint exercised by Farm Bureau leadership was nearly unique in pressure group history.
4. Interview with Rep. Cooley (D–N.C.).
5. *New York Times*, May 14, 1950, p. 7, col. 6.
6. Wesley McCune insisted that some hope was entertained that by changing the frame of reference from 90 per cent of parity in Title I of the Agricultural Act of 1948 to the concept of an "income support standard," a means was provided which would enable the Bureau, the Grange, and some Congressmen to retreat from their attachment to flexible price supports without too obviously repudiating their previous position. The strategy may have had possibilities, so far as individual Congressmen were concerned. Any examination of Farm Bureau literature during the early months of 1949, however, would make it seem highly improbable that Brannan could have anticipated such a development. The Secretary told me he was convinced that the Bureau was out to "get" him from the outset of his reappointment as Secretary of Agriculture. If he believed this, he could hardly expect the Bureau to follow his leadership on the crucial issue of price supports.
7. See Representative Cooley's comment on p. 174 above.
8. Representative Hope probably expressed the view of most farm Congressmen when he said: "We believe the question as to the level of price supports is one which must ultimately be determined by farmers be-

cause they are the ones who must live under such a program." *Congressional Record,* 81st Cong., 1st Sess., Vol. 95, Pt. 16, p. A5917.

9. E. A. Duddy, *Economic Policy for American Agriculture* (Chicago: University of Chicago Press, 1932), p. 3.

10. Who is responsible for a specific legislative act (or the failure to legislate) in the American political system? A House Congressional Committee? A Senate Committee? A Committee chairman? The Senate majority leader? The rules of the Senate? The Speaker of the House? A Congressional bloc? A Conference Committee? The Senate itself? The House? The Democrats? The Southern Democrats? The Republicans? The Old-Guard Republicans? The President?

11. Democratic National Committee, Publicity Division, R-623, June 13, 1949, p. 7.

12. Chairman J. Howard McGrath's early announcement in support of the Plan, which apparently set the committee machinery in motion, was made on his own initiative, McGrath reports. There seems to have been no awareness that this decision was a break with the past, or that it was an event of some importance in the history of American political parties. McGrath, viewing the Plan almost solely in terms of production payments and a free market for perishables, thought it would attract consumers as well as farmers, so he decided to give it a boost. He denies that either President Truman or Secretary Brannan urged him to take this step. (Information obtained by interview with Mr. McGrath.)

13. Wesley McCune wrote in 1943: "More than any other cabinet department, Agriculture is the protagonist, the pleader for its constituents. . . . Like the Department of Labor and the Department of Commerce, it grinds the axe officially for one part of the national economy—only more so." McCune, *The Farm Bloc,* p. 262.

14. Hardin, "The Politics of Agriculture in the United States," p. 573.

15. Even the Farmers Union, which supported 100 per cent of parity price supports, favored a benefits limitation which was far more stringent than Brannan's 1800-unit rule. The Farmers Union in 1949 would have limited support to that amount of produce which would enable farmers to net about $4,500. Brannan's limitation at least doubled the Farmers Union maximum.

16. O. V. Wells, in a discussion with the writer, noted that previous secretaries were generally more conservative on the question of price support levels than were the private farm organizations.

INDEX